Upstream

Mosquito, by the author and his grandchildren, 2021

Upstream

In the Alaska Wilderness

by

Eric Wade

SHANTI ARTS PUBLISHING
BRUNSWICK, MAINE

Upstream
In the Alaska Wilderness

Published by **Shanti Arts Publishing**

Cover and interior design by Shanti Arts Designs

Shanti Arts LLC
Brunswick, Maine
www.shantiarts.com

Photograph on cover and pages 1, 13, 33, and 149 by Diego Delso; Affluent of Nenana River, McKinley Park, Alaska; 2017; License CC-BY-SA

Interior photographs by Doylanne Wade and used with her permission

This book presents a truthful recollection of actual events in the author's life. Conversations have been recreated and/or supplemented. Claims made in the book are based on the author's experience, common knowledge, and a simple search of resources.

Printed in the United States of America

ISBN: 978-1-956056-20-4 (softcover)
ISBN: 978-1-956056-21-1 (digital)

Library of Congress Control Number: 2022930151

To Doylanne,

who has supported my dreams

for fifty years

Contents

Acknowledgements 9
Preface 11

May

Rose 14
Cabin 19
Insects 24
Killing Tree 30

September

River 34
Swans 39
Meadow 45
Spruce Hen 48
Owl 52
Wilderness Sounds 55
Other Senses 60
Shed 64
Impeller 69
Decisions 74
Moon 78
Rain Drops 81
Telling Time 84
Frost 91
Lynx 95
Be Careful 99
Wolves 102
Solitude 109
Cranberries 117
Night Time 120
Fire 125
Imagining the Worst 129
Calling Home 135
Bear on the Trail 142
Steinbeck 146

Going Home

Hourglass 150

Eric & Doylanne Wade 155

ACKNOWLEDGEMENTS

I'll start with the early readers who looked at this manuscript when it was still rough as a rocky river bottom: Wendy James, Jeff Ramseyer, Debra McKinney, Marsha Barnhart, James Wade, and Abby Kellner-Rode all read and commented on the first version. It was their ideas that eventually moved it along to a condition where publisher Christine Cote said "it sparked her interest." She's since provided significant editorial advice. Alaska authors Nick Jans, Dan Walker, Bill Sherwonit, Jeff Fair, and Tom Kizzia read the book when it reached a more complete stage and added additional suggestions. Their endorsements are included here. Nick Jans and Jeff Fair generously offered lengthy ideas that prompted me to think more carefully about what I was trying to say. Thanks to James Majetich and Elizabeth Heckel for insightful wilderness discussions and title ideas. My sons, Jack Wade, James Wade, Jed Wade, and Jake Wade, encouraged me, and my wife, Doylanne, who took all the interior photos in the book, was, as always, my final editor. Thank you all.

PREFACE

This little book took nearly three years from the first lines to publication. Not particularly noteworthy, I know, but I mention it because during those years I made six journeys to my homestead in Alaska's interior, and each trip proved more difficult than the one before. The most recent sojourn found Doylanne, my wife, and I with a broken motor, drifting five days on a freezing river before we reached a landing, perhaps the most trying river adventure we'd experienced in more than thirty years, which gets me to the point of this book: all of us must prepare for the most difficult times because with that grounding, we'll keep doing and going as we grow older. Afterall, we learn more when things go wrong.

We'll be going back soon.

Eric Wade
Wasilla, Alaska

May

1

Rose

She waited too long, should have burst out of there, not let the tiny points have their way. Now she lay prone in May roses, stuck with sickle-shaped prickles, and covered in bleeding blossoms. The gray river, the color of the sky, only a few slippery feet away, lapped over a submersed willow branch near her head. The main channel, eight feet deep, careened near the bank, the water temperature forty-five degrees. A grayling broke the surface with a gentle plop in front of the boat. I stood above her looking down. A couple rolls into the bushes and she ended in a wild salad with no way out that wouldn't hurt. Her left hand gripped ragged stems, or maybe it was the other way around. Her legs quivered. Her torso and head, soggy hay bales wrapped in twine, strained toward me. She laid in pink roses and cold rain.

"Doylanne, roll this way."

She unraveled uphill to her knees, clawed to the top of the incline, and screamed at the sky like I'd never heard from her while rain washed mud from her legs. Her echo crashed at us from across the river. She ran to the cabin, and I dashed to the boat and grabbed a tote of clothing. Minutes later we sat near the woodstove pulling rose prickles from her skin.

Through the front window, we watched the killing tree wave in the storm, a tree so named because it was sure to fall and slaughter someone one day. The decayed tree stood at the edge of the yard, eighty feet of pale, twisted spruce killed by fire. It leaned slightly toward the cabin, always moaning with the wind. Several times I'd stood at the base of this tree with a chainsaw so wary and uncomfortable I walked away. It had to go down this trip.

Four days before, Doylanne and I left town for our cabin. A couple pickups with trailers were parked at the launch, a quiet, buggy, and lonely stretch of sand. Dogs barked back in the trees at a cabin, the roof line visible. I pushed the boat into the current and putted away from the mosquitoes. The river ran dirty, a light brown coffee. May had been rainy, but now there was a pause, and the weather could go either way. I accelerated, and the boat rose slowly above the bow wave, reducing drag. We were soon planing; what's commonly referred to as being on step. Two hundred miles of river lay ahead. Doylanne smiled and handed me potato chips. The rain started in the afternoon and disguised the water surface. Screwing up meant crashing into a log or running aground on a sandbar or something ominous we hadn't yet experienced.

One hundred miles into the trip, the boat violently slid to a stop on a sandbar. I stepped off the boat, the water reaching above my ankles. Cold water, similar to a winter tap temperature at a northern home, might not be good for the heart, but what could I do? We were stuck in the middle of the river. It took twenty-four hours for us to push the boat free. That's the way it sometimes goes on these rivers. The twenty-two-foot flat-bottomed boat was loaded for a month's stay. To break free from the sand, I lifted the boat with a farm jack so water could run underneath, and we pushed the ton and a half of boat and supplies off the jack, moving the boat a few inches. Yes, an overweight aging man and his wife of forty-five years can push a lot of weight with the help of a river. After hundreds of dead lifts and squats by both of us, the boat floated again. I hurt a bit though. My sixty-six-year-old body looked like a gunshot hind quarter. Plavix was working. I drove the boat into an opaque sky dense with doubt for six more hours that afternoon. Water traps hid cleverly on every corner and clouds formed tunnels, luring me to enter, but I stayed along the high banks.

The fun had certainly run out of this river journey, but we finally made it. We pulled off the bear board covering the cabin door, a nasty shield of plywood and protruding nails, and started a fire in the stove. From the front window, I could see a million holes in the river surface. Cold rain bounced on the deck. We both stripped off wet clothing and stood in underwear near the woodstove that was beginning to make a difference. A quick dash to the boat, a few minutes, and we'd have a tote of dry clothing. "I'll do it," Doylanne said.

We needed the clothes. She paused on the deck before running toward the boat. At the bank's edge, she slipped and disappeared over the embankment. Rose vines held her horizontally suspended off the ground inches from the river. She screamed, a chilling screech sent to the river corners and into the woods to the ridges.

That's how she ended up dangling at the edge of the river.

Oh, roses. In Shirley Jackson's short story "The Possibility of Evil," the protagonist, the proper Miss Strangeworth, goes about life caring for her beautiful rose garden and outwardly showing love for the residents of her little town, a town built by her family where she's spent all but one day of her seventy-one years. She frequently leaves her treasured home, the first on Pleasant Street, and walks about encountering neighbors while evaluating their moods, speculating, and judging their lives. At home she writes hurtful letters, unsigned and on cheap colored paper, and mails them to her neighbors. The outwardly kind Miss Strangeworth was not what she seemed, much like a rose.

It didn't take long for us to get warm, but we'd be picking prickles for days. I'd never thought much about roses. I liked seeing them bloom in late spring. Now they were different to me and perhaps would always be. Doylanne now smiled, trying to make it funny. She was fine, she said. The apartment-sized propane stove fired up, so she made coffee and dinner. We would unload the boat after the storm passed. I watched the yard from the window. What about birch, willows, and highbush cranberries? I didn't think much about them either. They were just there. The whole place for that matter. I generally stayed away from diving too deep, thinking too much, but I was wondering more about calamities: the sweepers, sandbars, rose bushes, and sagging tree limbs smacking me in the face. I guess few places are more suitable for soul-searching and delving than beside a woodstove in a small log cabin. When will it be our turn to get smashed, pulverized, perhaps by a falling tree?

In bed, I listened to rain and the crackling fire and fell asleep staring into blackness harboring a growing discontent. I dreamt of a child's football game. On one sideline of the dirt lot was a concrete foundation left from the demolition of a derelict building filled with blackberry briars. I sprinted down the sideline racing for a touchdown when Mikey knocked me into the berry bushes. I lay there on my back, clutching the ball, thorns from the briars spearing my back and legs. I screamed, "Go get my Mom; go get my Mom." I woke still in the briars.

The rain stopped, and the wind, passing with powerful puffs, swept branches across the roof, making claw sounds. I hoped for nicer days ahead. Wind brings change. We'd waited a long winter, but now, finally mid-May, we were back to the forest and the cabin.

Morning steam rose from the deck, and a diamond necklace replaced the river. A red squirrel ranted from a nearby spruce, a tree so close to the deck that I'd trimmed the lower branches so we could more easily see bears in the yard. The trail to the boat dried and hardened with the heat and breeze. I emptied my wet pants onto the table: a wallet, small vial of nitro, truck keys, guitar pick, nail clippers, and two dollars and forty cents in change. Here I didn't need the coins and the few dollars I had. I put it all in a bowl except my wallet and vial of nitro, which ended up in my dry pants. I knew what my first job would be: with a machete, I would take care of the roses.

I climbed down the embankment to the gnarled briars with tattered pink petals and pulled them carefully apart. Those broken, I trimmed. A few I tied together with string to hold the vines standing. I pulled grass from around the base of the plants, aerating the soil to improve drainage and evaporation. I chopped down a few small willows to make room for the roses to spread. When I finished, I gathered a few petals to add to dinner.

Rose prickles impale other plants, impeding their growth. They dominate an area by monopolizing sunshine, a heartless action where there are so few months of sun. Kill them all, I thought, but wanted beautiful roses as did Doylanne, covering the river bank in red and pink petals. Emerson wrote, "the earth laughs in flowers," a good enough reason itself to care for roses, but there's another reason too. It's likely the hateful roses, beautiful deceivers they are, saved her life. She nearly rolled into the cold river on the deep side without a life vest.

We might need them again.

2

CABIN

THAT AFTERNOON I DRIFTED the river following grayling dimples, casting small flies into shadows along the edge. Doylanne chose to stay at the cabin. I wondered if we'd already experienced the best from this place, if it was time for us to stay in town and check the mail and gather the newspaper. I wondered a lot about that. I started the drift a few turns upriver and floated toward the cabin. At the stretch revealing the homestead, I stopped casting and looked. Back in the trees, obscured by reaching limbs and moving shadows, stood the log cabin and a few small buildings built from lumber taken from dead trees close enough to be hauled in my arms. The tip of the killing tree rose above it all. That little place, rising among herbs, mosses, shrubs, and sheltered by crowns of spruce and birch and shared with bears, moose, and dozens of other northern creatures, had oddly changed for me in a sad, ominous way, like someone I cared for lied to me, and I sat alone over a cup of coffee and wondered why. The landscape transformed from an adult playground of adventure and beauty to a mysterious and deceptive place. I imagined picking my way through the forest, brushing against roses and highbush cranberries, and stepping over fallen logs, like weaving down a busy city sidewalk with its arms and elbows. I reached for my wallet to ensure it was still there. In some puzzling manner, the place had altered its character.

In the evening, we sat on the deck in waning light, watching squirrels balance on spruce boughs.

"Doylanne, we might be too old."

She smiled like she does, cheeks lifting. "I don't know. Do you think?" Ah, I love her sarcasm.

"I wonder."

Chickadees flittered between the branches. The world in blue, an entirely different place than the rain-soaked realm of the day before, faded like a final movie scene. That's how days in May end, gradually, no abrupt curtain of darkness drawn across the forest stage.

May, when young bull moose prance on the river's edge and mosquitoes fly like balloons, is the most beautiful month in the boreal forest and the easiest to like. The land is the greenest green. Renewal explodes with an intensity obliterating the browns and grays leftover from winter. Beaming groundcovering plants and dense stands of birch and white spruce dominate the landscape. The growth is rapid because it must be. Spring lasts a few weeks, that's it, then it's on to summer when every day bends rapidly toward fall.

Leaf buds explode in May. It only takes a few days for them to burst to joyful green, quickly hiding the forest. Looking at the bank from the boat while passing a long stretch, the first impression is the black of the shadows, the gray of the spruce trunks, the blue-green of white spruce needles, the white of the birch trunks, and the Irish green of the new deciduous leaves. Animals hide easily behind the young summertime curtains.

This is the boreal forest of interior Alaska where I staked land in the 1980s and built a small homestead. I've voyaged to this place by boat nearly eighty times, the combined distance more than a circle of the earth. Doylanne traveled with me on most trips. The distance from home to the homestead and back is about one thousand miles, more than six hundred miles of narrow highway and approximately four hundred miles of river, like driving from Portland, Oregon, to Las Vegas—well, sort of. Our boat doesn't go as fast as an automobile.

We live two months a year in the trees along the river—May and September, the other easy month.

Well, easy enough.

"Going to make boards?" Doylanne asked.

"A tree's fallen near the outhouse. I'll get on it tomorrow."

I began logging and milling the next day, and it hurt. My chest burned as I knelt and sucked for air after trying to lift a twelve-foot spruce log onto a makeshift platform to saw a board. Faced with this task as a young man, I would have easily wrestled the log where it needed to go. I grabbed the peavey. The ashen colored log rolled nicely into place, but I still struggled for air. I drew on an inhaler. I used a tool when muscle should have worked, at least I wanted muscle to work. It hurt me a lot I couldn't lift the log.

An owl flew overhead. Maybe I was growing wise. Seems fair I'd get something for being around a long time. Certainly, my relationship with logs had changed through the years. I was reluctantly accepting that change.

With the log positioned, I scrubbed it with a wire brush and swept away the dirt. A beaver slapped not far upstream. I walked to the edge and watched the beaver mid-river coming my way. It slapped again and slipped below the surface.

Yes, I now look at logs differently; now they're heavy and ladened with memories.

I fueled up the chainsaw with oil-mixed gasoline and added bar oil. The log I faced came from a wind-blown spruce I'd bucked into four lengths. I counted the rings on a slice until I gave up after one hundred with still a long way to go. I had no regrets. It was dead when I found it. I'd probably get six boards, but there was work ahead, and the day was growing long. A big chainsaw with a twenty-five-inch bar and a saw mill makes a heavy load for old arms.

No doubt, wrestling a log hurts, sometimes a lot.

I finished with the log and stacked the boards. I planned to build a new outhouse for Doylanne so we'd have a his and hers. She wanted a hers. I also envisioned a new shed near the main cabin, shiplap floor and lap siding, built with white spruce, large enough to store all our gear and supplies—all of it, for us, our kids, grandkids, for the rest of time. The outhouse I would build in September. The shed, I wasn't sure when I'd get to it. We needed a shed, but I struggled with the idea some. Why does an old man need a new shed anyway? But I didn't like planning and talking and not doing. I drew in on the inhaler again and held my breath. The river moved serenely along, and an eagle swung away overhead. My chest dropped to a simmer. Clouds draped the trees, so I covered my tools with a tarp and meandered to the cabin, twisting my torso to relieve right-side pain. I changed out of my sweaty shirt and combed the sawdust from my hair.

For this day, my work was done. Doylanne handed me a glass of beer, and we went to the cabin deck to watch the river.

"Do you feel any prickles?"

"Yeah. A lot." There she goes again.

"Want me to look?" She shook her head.

A splash over the bank hidden by small willows made both of us smile, probably the same grayling I'd heard while she was tangled in briars.

"I don't want to go to town in June. Horns should be taken out of cars. Hasn't mankind moved beyond honking?" Doylanne smiled, her cheeks hiding her lower lashes, and pointed out two red-breasted mergansers coming downstream.

"We need to exercise at home," she said, grabbing the binoculars. "Are you going to hunt for moose in the fall?"

Moose hunting brushed a sore spot. The September before we both thought I might die lifting a moose into the boat.

"Probably."

"It might be time to quit that."

"Could be." I didn't much like killing things anyway.

I sipped my beer as ducks floated under a sweeper on the far bank. We sat back against the cabin logs as water lapped gently over submersed branches and birch leaves fluttered in the soft breeze.

"Look!" Doylanne pointed. A river of mayflies, hundreds of feet in length, wove upstream, undulating above the flowing mirror.

"Doylanne, we need to make this trip easier."

"How do we do that?" Grayling were showing across the river.

"At least think about it some. I'm going fishing. Coming?"

"No, I'll stay here and watch."

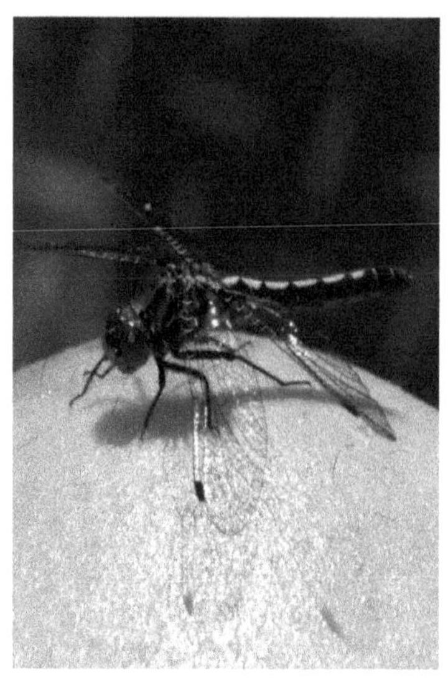

3

Insects

I caught one with a mosquito pattern, held it up so Doylanne could see and then let it go. Grayling acted like they hadn't eaten in a long while. I released a couple more before returning to the deck.

"Eric, you're right. We should start a list of ways to make this trip easier."

"I don't know if we can keep it up if we don't. Feels really different this year to me."

"How could it be different?"

"Feels like dodging bullets. How many bullets can we dodge?" I looked at her legs and the killing tree.

She waved an arm through the air. "Dragonflies need to get to work. How many mosquitoes can we dodge?" she said.

Ah, mosquitoes, besides the weather, the most powerful force in the boreal forest. By the end of May, they buzz and attack like they don't like you much. This did seem a bit early for them to be everywhere. Lots of other bugs buzzed and crawled about too. The bug diversity isn't great in the north, but those here are plentiful and determined. As for mosquitoes, insect repellent coils keep most of them hiding in the corners, but outside only the breeze and direct sun matter. Daily, I covered myself thoroughly with bug dope, and the bugs flew around and bounced off but never left. On the leeward side of the cabin or in the trees, the mosquitoes attacked in hordes.

"I'm going to walk out back," I said.

"Why?"

I headed to the ridge behind the cabin to a place I'd been many times. An animal trail meandered for a half mile before turning north up a gradual incline onto a ridge. There stood the tree I always leaned against. I added more repellent and scanned the vista.

To the south the top third of Denali dazzled; the rest was shrouded in clouds but for a strip of clear above the points of the tree tops. Denali floated. Moving eastward the green hills rose to an ultramarine sky. Closer, the tops of black-green white spruce crowns wove with the river. The river wasn't visible but gurgled below the spruce, its course easily followed by tracing the spruce. Further east another mountain, much smaller than those in the Alaska Range but standing alone, rose from the taiga.

I lit a repellent coil and a cigar. Smoke swirled, and mosquitoes flew through smoke rings. In a large meadow below me, hawks hunted—circling and diving. I watched with binoculars until falling asleep beneath a tree, waking an hour later, an arm covering my head shielding me from bugs. A cow moose stood in the tall grass. Alone, it grazed at the edge of the small pond, looking up every few moments, its ears—round-pointed digging shovels—stood erect. It turned and walked into the trees. I swung the repellent coil around my head to infuriate flying bugs.

Sometimes beauty sucks the energy from you. I couldn't move, stuck against my old friend the tree, the view before me, as the clouds blew beyond Denali, literally breathtaking. So I sat another hour swatting mosquitoes and peering with binoculars into the woods at the edge of the meadow.

A mosquito filled itself with blood. I watched it. It landed on my left wrist. It must have found a tolerable spot. It hunkered down and soon I saw it begin to fill. A red balloon on my wrist expanded. It didn't hurt. I'd already been pierced by so many proboscises—six thin, tiny needles, the mosquito's weapon—I didn't feel this one having the meal of its life. I watched and hoped it gorged itself to death. I didn't move. One minute passed. Another. I imagined it paused, a moment of sanity, and realized it was doomed. I lightly brushed it away, and it lifted off, barely flying, an overloaded, overfilled glutton soon to crash and spill my blood.

Mosquitoes weren't the only insect sitting with me. At my feet ants swarmed a rotten log. I kicked the log and a long swath of bark peeled away, and hundreds of ants spread like BBs spilled on a floor. Ants exist in the millions. Researchers believe there once was a time when the biomass of ants equaled humans on earth. Apparently that view has been altered since the human population explosion of the twentieth century, but it's likely still close. In Brazil it's thought the biomass of ants exceeds that of all the land vertebrates in the region—all the king vultures and river turtles and everything else, combined. Here at the homestead, it seems a fair guess Doylanne and I were outnumbered and outweighed.

These ants, *Hymenoptera: Formicidae*, carpenter ants, live in communities with three castes: the queen, which lays eggs and never leaves the nest; swarmers, large females and smaller males, with wings; and lastly, workers. Queens and workers have pretty specific duties, but swarmers are the flying daredevils responsible for the perpetuation of the species. Swarmers spring upward from communities in the spring and fly. During flight, ants copulate. The males die shortly after, but the females, now mated for life and fertilized, reestablish old community sites and develop new sites in stumps or logs. The female rips off her wings and becomes the queen and begins laying eggs. The queen can reign for up to fifteen years. Fifteen years! The eggs hatch after a little more than three weeks, and the larvae, resembling grubs too nasty to touch, morph to the pupal stage and eventually, after another three weeks, become ants, some of them workers and some swarmers. All eggs produced by the queen in the first three years are sterile female workers. When you see ants at work, you are seeing females. They excavate, tend to eggs, gather food, and generally look after the queen.

Wilderness and solitude are synonymous, but ants,

everywhere in the wilderness, are the antithesis of solitude. They live in communities, in colonies; they work together, eat together, and die together. There are no lone ants searching for self or harboring delusions of grandeur. They work as a team, and they outnumber mankind 1.5 million to one.

In Carl Stephenson's "Leningen Versus the Ants," the owner and leader of a large Brazilian plantation is warned to leave his plantation immediately because of an advancing horde of ants. Leningen refuses and the ants reach his land where an epic battle ensues. Both man and ants display strength and toughness, and both exhibit matching intelligence. It just so happens, like in most stories, Leningen has one last desperate move before doom, and it succeeds. Many of his men perished, but he survived, gravely injured. It's quite clear, though, that Leningen got lucky. "Before you can spit three times, they'll eat a full-grown buffalo to the bones," Stephenson wrote in his story.

I wiped the ants from my boots and stood. I had one more place I wanted to see. I hiked further up the hillside, picking my way through roses and stepping over fallen trees. I came to an opening made by my sons and me nearly thirty years before. Not much of an opening now, but I could see the evidence: rotten tree stumps and scarred trees where we blazed a line. This was the township line, the boundary line for our property. If I walked north, I would reach a meadow the size of a city. I brought one beer. I reapplied repellent and sat on a fallen tree. A mosquito flew in my mouth and was swallowed with a drink.

Mosquitoes develop in water, not beer, and not in a cesspool of a stomach like mine, so I wasn't worried. I'd swallowed lots of them. Mosquitoes form from an egg and can morph to an adult in five days. An adult mosquito is an attractive flying machine. With translucent wings and sleek body, it floats when it wants and zips when it needs. Some of them carry diseases that kill millions but not Alaska mosquitoes. They mostly only pester. Sometimes, though, they bother to the point of being a serious problem.

Their ferociousness is legendary. Stories from construction workers on the Alaska Highway and soldiers during WWII make skin crawl.

Sometimes if I sit still, I can kill a dozen with one swipe across a thigh, and sometimes I wonder about killing so many. In the short story "The Adventure of a Young Mosquito" by Anglea Mathal, a young boy mosquito leaves home to explore the world. His parents worry but let him go. Eventually he returns home after various adventures and after concluding that home is where he belongs.

The day slid away like old friends sometimes do. Time to go back. I hiked to the cabin, retracing my route and watching mosquitoes rise off ponds. Mosquito eggs float on the surface of water, some singly form rafts. Some eggs are laid in wet soil soon to be flooded. Typically, the eggs will hatch to larvae within forty-eight hours. Larvae live in water and go to the surface to breath, which is odd to me. I don't think of a mosquito larva needing to breathe. But they do. They hang upside down at the surface with snorkels. They shed their skin a few times while eating tiny things until they change to a pupa. The pupa is the cocoon stage. In this stage, the mosquito-to-be doesn't do much. It mostly rests until it emerges a few days later as a satin winged little boy or girl.

We ate dinner inside the cabin, watching the river from a window. Birds were singing and undoubtedly feasting on little mosquitoes testing their wings. I checked on the burning repellent coils smoldering in the cabin. One was near the door in a small camping pan pushed against the log wall, the other below the side window facing the river. We went to bed early.

Sometimes I'm awake before my eyes open and lay there and keep them closed, hoping to fall back asleep. That night, a mosquito buzzed near my face. It probably woke me. I blindly waved it away, pulled blankets over my head, and listened to the buzz, enjoying the feeling of melting into the sheets, resting while the enemy expended energy. The mosquito stayed above me. I could track its flight pattern, back and forth, away for a few moments, back and forth. I swatted at it again and missed. Persistent little guy wasn't going away.

Hours later I opened my eyes. Several mosquitoes buzzed noisily above my head. Black under the covers, I couldn't see, but something lingered. I pulled the cover off and sat up and turned on the flashlight. Smoke rolled from the spruce log above the insect repellent coil near the door.

I jumped out of bed and kicked the small pan away from the wall and poured coffee water on the log.

"What's going on?" Doylanne asked.

"Dodging mosquitoes, Doylanne. Damn it. We damned near caught the damn place on fire."

We couldn't sleep after that.

4

Killing Tree

The river lay smothered in translucent vapor, a long gray wall starting at the water's edge and rising to blend with the light haze above. At ground level near the cabin, visibility was good. I could see the killing tree standing over us. With no wind, it was time for the tree to be laid to rest.

I'd felled dozens of trees and knew a decayed tree posed special dangers, particular those standing mostly straight. They don't always land where you want, and they sometimes explode. This insipid tree was clearly dead, all bark long ago fallen away, twisting cracks, broken limbs, some hanging, many scattered about its base.

I cleared around the tree and made an escape route to sprint away before starting the first horizontal cut. The eighteen-inch bar on my saw couldn't reach fully across the trees so I sawed a few inches alternating sides so the cut was made as close to the same time as possible. A tree reacts as soon as it's cut. A live tree has the strength to be predictable, not so a dead tree. I sawed about a fifth of the way through the twenty-four-inch trunk, followed with a diagonal cut through decay and worm holes. I knocked out the slice leaving an open mouth. On the opposite side of the mouth, I started a horizontal cut about four inches above the corner of the mouth on the side across from the direction I wanted the tree to go and drove a wedge in the cut. Then I sawed the other side to connect the cut. I drove a wedge a short distance on that side. After knocking out the first wedge, I cut deeper and replaced the wedge before removing the second wedge.

Now the tree had a mouth cut on one side and on the back side a horizontal cut across the full trunk with a wedge ready to be driven to help direct the fall. The tree was about to go. Doylanne watched from the cabin deck. I circled the tree and it smiled at me.

I drove the wedge further and the tree moved in the right direction and stopped. I stepped back and waited. It wasn't moving. I sawed into the tree another couple inches, and the tree settled in the wrong direction. It was as straight as when I began. Not good. I hammered the wedge more and the tree moved again toward where I wanted it to go. It was close, but it wasn't committed. I wished I'd gone a little deeper with the cut where the wedge was driven. I was wary, though, of cutting deeper. The idea is not to cut all the way through a tree. The best control is when the tree breaks at the pivot, an area ideally four inches above the corner of the mouth. I used a heavy splitting maul as another wedge, and the tree moved and cracked. I ran back the escape path and watched. I didn't think it would hit the cabin but it now seemed possible. I hollered to Doylanne to go to stand near the woodshed. We waited and waved to one another. Leaves along the river began to flash.

Damn I screwed up. I didn't saw deep enough. I ran back to the tree and gave the maul another good whack and sprinted away.

And waited.

The fog began to clear and the river came into view. The breeze from the east rapidly turned the river surface ragged. Leaves fluttered, first slightly, followed by a rustle. A loud crack and the tree went down, perfectly.

We headed home the second week of June. We circled before the cabin like we always do when leaving, dreaming ahead. We'd be back in September.

September

5

River

In September I left for the wilderness with a goal: This journey would mark a reset, a rediscovery of the wild country, the northern boreal forest, and a reckoning of my place in it, certainly an ostentatious goal, but a necessary one.

Doylanne and I woke on the river with still one hundred miles to go. We laid awake in our sleeping bags. "Have any dreams?" I asked. Days often started recalling a dream.

"We were at a railroad station. I think King's Cross. Just arrived from the subway, trying to get to the wedding. All of us were there: all the boys and daughters-in-law and grandchildren. The place was packed. We were swept along with the mass of people, and I didn't think we were being pushed to the right gate. I screamed to change course, but we had no choice. People ahead of us were pushed through a narrow doorway. There was no stopping. I'm glad I woke up. I usually don't have nightmares."

"Ready for coffee?" I asked.

The rain rang on the boat cabin roof. She moved first.

A bent finger, one I'd broken that summer and now needed to pump the portable gasoline cookstove, throbbed. My hands, with their mauve veins, ached. I pumped thirty-five times, the magic number, and carefully placed the gas tank in the stove. I smelled gasoline and heard the hiss of escaping fluid. A narrow stream sprayed onto my raincoat. There it was, a pin-sized hole in the fuel tank. The gasoline arched at me like a little boy peeing off a balcony. I rapidly pulled the tank from the miserable, rusty stove. My old friend of more than thirty years, abused like a cheap knife, failed me. I thought it'd live forever.

Doylanne and I wanted easy coffee. With a thermos, we'd head upriver through the morning fog and drizzle toward the homestead and eat a few fig bars. That was the plan.

I hadn't counted on a faulty fuel tank, although I should have. Now we had a choice. Skip coffee or build a fire in the rain and heat the water. We did our chores to get ready to leave. Doylanne shoved her sleeping bag into its pouch, hung it on a hook in the boat cabin, and started on mine.

I held the stuff bag and she pushed until I took over.

"Can you think of anything good that follows a hiss?" I asked.

She scrunched her face. She wasn't ready for stabs at humor, yet. "Not off hand, Eric. Can you fix the stove?"

Not going to happen. My liquid fuel gasoline stove, developed in 1902 by William Coffin Coleman in Wichita, Kansas, had died.

I walked briskly down the beach gathering firewood and calculating time. Ten hours of daylight remained in the day with the homestead about seven hours away if all went well. If there were problems, we'd camp another wet night along the river. Doylanne joined me, and we built a funeral pyre with wet wood. I made a torch by cutting the top off a pop can and filling it half way with gasoline. Poof! Flames rolled up the inside of the can walls producing a strange controlled dynamic, one I now expected after having performed this trick dozens of times—by the way, one not to be attempted around anything you don't want burned down. A fire crept to life. I found dead willows in the woods, mostly out of the rain, shielded by a thick willow leafy canopy. After a bit, I set the ten-cup metal coffee pot in the flames, propped against the largest sticks. The fire eventually took off, flames and sparkles reaching waist-high, white ashes fading into the wet pearl sand. We both used long sticks to poke at the coals and reposition the wet wood, circling to avoid the smog. When we finished, I buried the fire's remains. We'd become accustomed to the cookstove and weren't prepared to build a fire for coffee. I wasn't ready for a piece of equipment to fail. To build a fire in the rain, albeit, with a gasoline-fueled torch to ignite the wet wood, posed an inconvenience we hadn't faced in recent years. We did, though, have fresh water, so there was no need to boil it, only get it hot. An hour later we were on our way with a full thermos and steaming cups of coffee fogging the windshield.

How important was coffee?

Our expectations were high, an appetite well established. Preconditions for success and comfort that included morning coffee were set during years of wilderness excursions and always sealed and delivered one way or another. Or put another way, we were pretty much addicted to coffee. The caffeine rushed to our brain, lifting our spirits, lightening our mood, and researchers say maybe even making us a bit smarter, temporarily. As we settled into our coffee and small talk, all was good and safe.

Doylanne stirred in canned milk and placed a cookie on a napkin on the dash. "Is the coffee okay?" she asked.

"Good. You look pretty this morning." She glanced at me unconvinced and shook her head and smiled.

"I like the mornings."

We loved the cold together, pulling our knit hats over our ears, wiping condensation from the windows, and occasionally holding hands. Doylanne and I are usually relaxed on the river. We'd learned how. The bed in the boat took us years to figure out and was a triumph over tents on the beach or cold boat bottoms. The night before, wolves, obviously near us, howled, but we were fine. We believed we had control. As we cruised upriver, we talked about kids, books, dreams, paintings, poems, and new building projects at the homestead. We were relaxed and happy, and we linked coffee to satisfaction. Could Doylanne and I have achieved our outcome without coffee? I don't know.

We moved steadily up the delicate ribbon into the foothills on the north side of the Alaska range until I ran the boat onto a sandbar. On a sharp curve, I crossed the river but slightly missed the channel, the starboard side grinding to a stop in the sand. I went to the bow and the boat moved a little.

"Stay in the boat, Eric."

I leaned into the pole, and the boat slid back into the channel.

We cruised on our way again. The early September deciduous trees glowed. We knew this place, the river and the ridges, and the distant mountains well enough to run through it comfortably. We worked hard through the years to make the trip peaceful, or at least usually so. Our twenty-two-foot flat-bottomed boat with an aluminum cabin in the stern was a recreational vehicle powered by a large four-stroke outboard motor capable of pushing a two-thousand-pound load on step. The boat cabin's large glass windows, windshield wipers, heaters, fans, floor mats—all details we didn't have in the early years—resulted in a tiny home.

We were content on the river, sometimes even close to its flow. Many of us feel connected to a river I suspect: Yukon, Porcupine, Kenai, Kuskokwim, Innoko, Noatak, Naknek, Nushagak, Tanana, Susitna, Koyukuk are all turbulent rivers with beautiful names tumbling to the ear. There are more than twelve thousand rivers in Alaska, about two thousand of them still unnamed. It may seem peculiar, but I was first moved to write about our river in interior Alaska after spending an hour gazing at the Hudson River from Riverside Park while Doylanne and I were visiting our son Jed who lived on 116th street in Manhattan. The Hudson flowed before us. I couldn't hear it—the city pounded around me—but its beauty was undeniable. I wondered what this river, the home to both Lenape and Algonquin for thousands of years, was like before European migration. What sights and sounds of wilderness did Henry Hudson stumble upon in the *Half Moon*? Millions have loved this river. I loved it at first sight. "Rivers naturally all have their little ways," wrote Constance Helmericks in *Down the Wild River North*. Yes, indeed, and many people have bonded, sometimes metaphysically, to those natural ways. I once conducted a personal exercise to test this hypothesis. "What river do my friends love?": Steve, down in Oregon, grew up fishing the Alsea; Louie hunted frogs along the Yaquina; Paul and Helen lived yards from Willow Creek; Doug fished the Kuskokwim; Buddy stalked steelhead on the Siletz; and Mike floated the Little Willow. Friends with river memories were everywhere: one friend lived by a river, canoed its water, and fished in its rapids; one worked on a river as a youth, guided logs to the mill, and worked as a deck hand on a barge; another dreamed of a high-rise apartment in the Upper West Side of Manhattan from which to watch the Hudson. One I know says he fell in love while rafting the Yukon, and one spent a life on the Wabash River, water most certainly pumping through his veins. Many of us entertain a special fondness for a river, a pillow we pull close and fall asleep to memories of its sound.

6

Swans

In the afternoon the sky merged with the river; the horizon disappeared, and we ran toward the edge of a flat world. Trees along the bank, many horizontal, others fallen into the water, a few slumped by the downpour, became hidden in the rain and foggy glass. The wipers only cleared a small slice of the windshield. I squinted to see a river surface resembling cold skin. Enough. I couldn't see, and it was obvious we wouldn't get to the homestead before dark. I anchored to a long, soaked beach. We crawled into our sleeping bags before dark and listened to the rain dancing on aluminum. Water poured and rivulets ran down the center of the floor. Our boatel floated under an open faucet.

"Will you be able to sleep?" I asked Doylanne.

"Yes, I like it."

"You like it?" I had been thinking about her dream all day. "About your dream, I don't have nightmares either."

"I like the sound of the rain on the cabin roof. I'll have good dreams."

I wasn't sure I liked the drubbing, not enough for good dreams. A lot of water dropped on us, but it stopped in the night. The silence was the first thing I noticed when I woke, followed by my sleeping arms and aching back. I turned in the sleeping bag and looked up through the glass windows to stars. The sky shone brighter at night than during the day in the rain. I nudged Doylanne.

"Look."

The sky had donned a rhinestone jacket.

Directly overhead a droplet of water clung to the cabin ceiling, a product of water vapor to liquid water. When it fell, it would hit me in the face. I waited until it did, a drop traveling through time since the earth's beginning.

I started a campfire in the morning for coffee, the sky a hazy white. We both stood near the fire, away from the smoke and took deep breaths. It's said the purest air in the world is in the Finnish Lapland at the 67th Parallel. Doylanne and I stood on the 64th in Alaska. Good enough. We both went to the boat for more layers of clothing, the temperature in the high thirties. The day would warm to the sixties.

"Good dreams?" I asked.

"I don't remember any. So I guess that's good. You?"

"Yeah, tell you later if I remember it."

"How much farther?"

"Probably fifty miles."

We left with our coffee and fig bars and small piles of morning medication, and soon the sun warmed the boat cabin, so we opened the cabin door and the air hit us straight on, first a little cold and minutes later uncomfortably perfect like after scratching a bad itch. On one river corner a pair of swans pounded their way into the sky.

"Swans never wait for us," she said.

I'd noticed as well. They led the way on every trip. More than 80 percent of the world's trumpeter swans, the largest waterfowl, spend summers in Alaska, many near the cabin. When not in view of the river, they float on nearby lakes honking and slapping wings. Nothing in the boreal forest is like a swan. Doylanne always dashes for the camera. A pivotal time for the survival of swans is late fall when young birds called cygnets, having survived raptors, pike, lynx, and wolves, must fly before freeze up. The September beforc, Doylanne and I saw a swan pair with three cygnets on a small lake near the cabin. We watched them practice take-offs on the tightly rippled water. It didn't seem to be going well; the little ones couldn't get off the water. They ran the runway and tried but couldn't pull away. We went back several times to the lake over a three-week period to silently cheer them on, usually during the hours before dusk, and they were always there on the shallow gun-barrel-blue water, until a cold evening when they weren't. On our way back to civilization, cruising on the river near a long beach of ivory colored sand, we saw a swan family of five. The two white adults took off away from us downstream, immediately followed by the three ashen cygnets. All rose off the water and banked over the trees. We pointed and smiled, imagining our family of swans on its long journey south.

About noon we pulled to the bank at the homestead. Before us our cabin, woodshed, outhouse, and guest cabin (place to put stuff) sat among the trees. We walked around it all, comparing it to how we left it in June, before hauling our gear and supplies onto shore. Exhausted, I stretched and reached for my shoes and made it to my shins.

"It's always beautiful." She sat on the cabin deck. "I can't wait for the new outhouse and the shed."

I hung a basket of flowers brought from town. A bright golden circle held a spot on the water in front of us, the sun near the tips of the trees to the southwest.

"I'll get to the outhouse, not sure of the shed."

"You okay?"

A pair of pintails landed in the river.

The sun disappeared behind a supersonic cloud, and a shadow fashioned a short-lived strip across the river where the golden circle faded. A mother duck with five adolescent ducklings slipped into the shadow for a journey to the other side. I sat up to watch this adventure, immediately concerned for the duck family. Eagles and ospreys regularly float over the river looking for a meal. What's a better meal than a duckling?

"Stupid," I said. Doylanne watched with binoculars. The ducks paddled purposefully but were painfully slow. I watched the sky. It took a couple minutes, but they reached the edge, disappearing under sweepers upstream. This mother exposed her tender morsels to the open sky. A row of baby ducks looked like an easy target paddling behind mom. The ducks lingered at the edge weaving in and out of sweepers. I sat back. Doylanne and I had completed the journey, despite a near coffee emergency and poor visibility. We'd made it again like the little ducklings.

The cabin is located south of the Yukon River, roughly the center of the state. The route runs southwest toward the north side of the Alaska range and Denali, which is often visible. There are four rivers to navigate to get to the homestead. The rivers are part of a large glacial system encompassing thousands of miles along the Yukon River. The rivers are braided and difficult to navigate, particularly during low water periods, which are variable and unpredictable. The rivers change dramatically between May and September, the months when they flow ice free. The waters, which warm up to about forty-five degrees in the summer, are Class 1 with current speeds under ten miles per hour, but sweepers, trees lying in the water, run the entire course. Spears pointing downstream positioned ten to fifty feet from the bank, peek out from the frigid surface during high water and stand out like lances when the river runs low.

River trips are usually cold even in the summer when the sun in the interior blazes. On the warmest day, sometimes in the eighties, it's cold in an open boat. Get on the river and run twenty miles an hour, and it's immediately autumn. Run twenty miles an hour in mid-August and you'll believe you're freezing. Run twenty miles an hour in late September in an open boat and you might freeze.

I sat on the deck and fiddled with the portable cookstove while Doylanne readied the cabin. She positioned antique brass bed warmers now used as holders for insect repellent coils at strategic places; cleaned the counter tops and the propane cook stove; inspected the nooks and crannies for invasions of mice or squirrels; made the bed; swept the floor; stocked the cupboards. It didn't take long to get the cabin ready.

"Eric, can you bring up water?"

We'd overcome the failed camp cookstove easily enough, perhaps, but it bothered me. I imagined failures resulting in much bigger problems.

"I might find a welder to plug the hole in this old tank."

"We've had it forever. We need a new one."

"Maybe, but I want this one."

"We need two stoves."

She was right. We needed a backup, but not another gasoline stove. If we ran shy on fuel, we'd be out of luck. A four-hundred-mile river trip with a large outboard takes a lot of fuel. For a month-long trip, I usually carried one hundred fifty gallons of gasoline, and we usually ran low. Once, years before, I ran out of fuel in sight of the launch, fortunately close enough to get to a bank and walk to town. We needed a different kind of stove.

We discussed options through the afternoon, and before evening I built a biomass stove to use on the way home. I cut a hole in the side of an empty gallon paint can I found in the shed, and I cut the ends off an evaporated milk can and pushed it into the side of the paint can. I cut an arching notch in the bottom side of a fruit cocktail can to match up with the evaporated milk can. The last step: I poured sand into the paint can so it all didn't fall over. There it was—a biomass stove. The stove worked by starting a fire in the side hole with leaves and twigs and adding small wood pieces from both the side and the top. The fire channels up the fruit cocktail can.

"This'll get us home. There I'll buy a good one."

I resolved to have two ways to heat water. Redundancy was not a new idea for me, but coffee drove its importance home. Water pump kits, spark plugs, and propellers all need backups—the basic definition of redundancy—but there's another level. Redundancy is also identifying more than one way to complete a task, a definition fitting cook stoves, siphoning hoses, porta-potties, and frankly, most needs. We needed to rethink our supply and equipment list.

A September evening arrives with little notice. We sat on the deck discussing redundancy and decisions while ducks played hide and seek beneath the sweepers. The river dropped during the day. A beach grew downriver.

"Doylanne, we have fewer bad dreams as we age."

"Are you still thinking about my dream?"

"I think bad dreams pull us to earth, hold us back some, keep us in our place. When we're old, we have no place to go, little to do, so no need for them anymore."

"Don't know, Eric. Pretty negative."

"Bad dreams are warnings, so they can be good."

She smiled.

"I remember the dream I had about my grandparents last night. I've been having them lately."

"Tell me."

"The street at intown Grandma and Grandpa's house ended at a town-size cornfield. I ran into the cornfield, all the corn stocks towering over me, and ate baby corn. It tasted like candy and might have been my first awareness of wrong. I knew the corn wasn't mine or Grandma or Grandpa's. So I tried to hide the evidence by brushing off my shirt, but I got caught. Grandma could smell it. She didn't scold me, but she would say, 'You go out in a big cornfield, you'll get lost one day.' And I did. I couldn't help myself. I stumbled through the maze until breaking through the corn stocks to the banks of a big river. Fishermen in a small boat waved at me. It was the Ohio River not far from its confluence with the Wabash."

"We should go there someday," she said.

The beach downstream from the cabin revealed itself nearly every trip, creating a bridge spanning most of the river. A game trail led to the beach, and moose often used the pathway to get to the river and cross. We angled our chairs toward the beach. A red squirrel bounded among the branches in the spruce near the deck, throwing cones at us. We sat in the wilderness near the center of Alaska waiting for a wildlife show to begin.

"Doylanne, let's not do stupid stuff on this trip."

"Okay."

7

Meadow

Wolves sang as the sun slid near the tips of the spruce. Doylanne heard them first. Snips, snarls, and howls, and another group joined from the north behind the cabin. Call and response like blues guitarists. We sat with wolves; the cirrus laden skies whirred with howls. The wolf song went on for several hypnotic minutes with brief breaks. During pauses the cool breeze filtered through the leaves, holding our attention as we looked to the horizon waiting, and a wolf would again start the music. When it was over, fluttering leaves took over again, bustling and flashing in the last hour of daylight.

"I'm going to walk toward Jake Lake. Might see a moose before wolves eat them all. Be back before dark."

"Getting late. You sure?"

"Be back in an hour."

"Don't shoot a moose."

I grabbed a rifle and backpack and entered the trees, weaving through an audience of wild peeping Toms. I'd covered myself with bug dope as strategically placed as Lady Godiva's hair. A trail ran behind the trees a half mile upriver, passing a small body of water we called King Beaver Pond.

At the north end of the water, against a bank leading to a ridge of black spruce and tundra, stood a massive beaver lodge. I turned off the trail northward into a thick stand of spruce, picking my way over fallen trees and around sink holes filled with black water. Several minutes or so into the trees, I heard a crash to my left. I knelt and looked through the understory with binoculars. I moved toward the sound. A few steps and stop. A few more and stop. I kept on this pace, a squirrel ranting ahead of me, until I heard an exhale. I stopped and waited at a jumble of collapsed spruce and a swath of fire debris. I skirted charcoaled logs laying crisscrossed. The trees thinned ahead, and I could see the growing light of a meadow. No moose. I sat at the edge of the opening, my back against a tamarack.

I was already mad at myself. I wouldn't get back to the cabin before dark. The light goes so quickly in the trees. Moonlight and flashlight would have to get me home. A couple hawks hunted the meadow, weaving between the darkness near trees and the remaining light over the meadow. The golden needles of tamaracks marked the edge.

Stars faded in and out like outdoor Christmas lights in a breeze. I unzipped my coat and wiped sweat. I'd followed the moose too far.

Using a GPS, I headed toward the cabin. The triangle icon didn't move. After a few minutes I wasn't sure. This didn't feel right. I'd been hiking gradually uphill, but now I wasn't going downhill. I kept going, picking my way, my visibility limited to the narrow band of my flashlight through an alder thicket, all black except for the narrow beam. When I broke through, starlight shone through the trees. I should have made it to the river by now. A wolf howled and others joined. I stopped next to a large spruce and turned off the flashlight and stood in pitch black, backpack and rifle on the ground in front of me. I turned slowly looking for a light from the cabin. Nothing. Doylanne would have the gasoline lantern going and be worried by now. She would stand at the cast iron porcelain sink and step out to the deck, listening to the wolves, staring into the blackness. Ours is a snaky river. Standing in place, I circled again, eyes closed, listening for a clank at the cabin. Maybe I'd walked too far to the east and missed the river. The river curved to the south not far from the cabin. Maybe I moved parallel with it. Possibly. If I was walking south, I would eventually reach the river because the river would curve again. Trust the GPS, I told myself; of course you're walking south.

When I staked the property in 1987, I didn't have a GPS. It wasn't until 1983 that GPS became available for civilians, but the early technology was too expensive for me. Standing in the woods in the dark, I knew it worked, but I still didn't trust it. Don't be silly, I told myself; follow the GPS.

Five minutes later at another opening I rested. I could be walking away from the river. A waxing moon and the stars lit the small meadow. Should I fire the rifle? Doylanne would hear it, probably, but would she understand I wanted her to make noise, maybe shoot the shotgun standing in the corner near the rear window. Maybe I should yell out, but would she think I was a wolf. Would the wolves think I was a wolf? Would the wolves think I was a meal?

Two walkie-talkies were in the boat, not yet unpacked because I'd spent my time building a biomass stove because my cook stove died. It was the stove's fault. A shooting star flashed near the horizon. If I could find the Little Dipper and the tip of its handle, Polaris, the northern star, I could walk away from it and be heading south. Stars were out, but I wasn't sure, astronomy not a strong suit. I checked the GPS and kept going. I slipped and fell onto a spruce, my face hitting first. I ended on my back. Feet were okay, knees okay. I surveyed my body, working from my toes upward. All okay except my face began to sting, from my right-side ear to my chin. I laid there, gulping air. The wolves started up again. I rolled to my knees, stood, and lunged into the trees. I tripped again, falling into a sinkhole. My right arm sank in water but stopped me from rolling entirely into the basin. I rolled onto my back and again stopped to breathe. Man. The trees don't care. Here, only Doylanne and I cared whether or not I made it. I rolled up the incline away from the water and stood. Slow down. This is easy. Go south.

Exhausted, I met the river a short distance from the cabin. I hollered at the edge of the trees and took my time catching my breath, crossing the clearing. The cabin smelled like cookies.

8

Spruce Grouse

The coals in the enamel-coated cast-iron woodstove dawdled. The thermometer on the nightstand read forty-four degrees. I didn't want to get out from the covers. I squinted to read Doylanne's grandmother's ticking Big Ben wind-up alarm clock. Outside, wind chimes rang and the polyurethane curtain on our outdoor shower flapped. I rolled out of bed and started heating water in an old aluminum coffee pot.

"Not too smart last night. You always go out when we first get here." Doylanne pulled herself up and rested against the cabin logs with blankets pulled to her chin. Her brown eyes looked up from her coffee. "I had a dream you drowned. You were in the river and I couldn't get to you. I couldn't move. I tried to reach, but my body wouldn't budge. I tried to scream but nothing. You disappeared under the water. Then you surfaced and floated away."

"I hate those dreams when you can't move," I said. I poured coffee and stoked the stove and cracked open a couple windows. "A pretty weird dream."

"What happened, Eric?"

"I have to stop doing stupid stuff." Her cheeks lifted.

"Why start now? What's on your face? If you get hurt, you won't be able to do the projects you've been planning."

I checked the mirror. I looked like I'd slid across asphalt.

"I hit a tree. Doylanne, does it feel different to you, this trip?"

"You've already asked that. What's the bruise on your shoulder?"

"Plavix. Every other step, I trip over something."

"Being out in the dark doesn't help. Let's make a list of things not to do."

"Not funny. I followed a moose. What else could I do?"

She shook her head and stared at her coffee.

I made bacon and eggs, mixed pancake batter in a yellow Pyrex refrigerator dish, and Doylanne watched a granddaughter on a video saved on her phone. I climbed down the bank to the boat and watched two swans on a beach downstream. They stood facing each other, necks waving. I imagined talking.

Back in the cabin, I rambled. "Doylanne, sound decision-making is a problem for aging people. Maybe that's me. I don't know."

"It's not age, Eric."

"There's so much one must know to make good decisions, but where's the information? We don't know that much. Not really. Information is people lying."

"Lying?"

"When we were young, it didn't matter if we were right. We could be close and that worked. If we made a mistake, we had time to fix it. If we break a leg now, the healing time may take the rest of our lives."

"You're over-thinking it. You got lost."

"I know. Stupid, spur of the moment decision. Isn't that a teenage problem? It's an old person problem too. It was dangerous. Considering pain might have worked. If I would have considered falling into the tree, I might not have left the cabin so near dark. I respect pain. Pain hurts. I should tell myself: stay in the boat; wear a life jacket; don't run a chainsaw when tired; don't pee out of the boat; carry an emergency pack; don't go hunting near dark; get home in daylight; keep batteries charged; check CO_2 alarms; don't lean the rifle against a tree; don't lean against the gas range reaching for spices; don't spill gasoline on the deck; don't forget your medicine. Is there any coffee?"

Doylanne slowly raised her head and smiled. "I don't think age is to blame. You've always gone out in the woods near dark."

I worked near the cabin gathering firewood, parking out the woods, hauling small brittle branches and tree relics to the old cabin spot and potential firewood to the woodshed, all slow deliberate decisions in daylight where I could be seen. I wandered blindly in the dark the night before perhaps toward a gingerbread cottage and a boiling pot. Hansel and Gretel's bread crumbs wouldn't have led me home. There is no end to the boreal forest.

By early afternoon I sat on the deck tinkering with the biomass stove. A few feet from me, a spruce grouse hopped and grabbed a high-bush cranberry. The lowest berries, ruby freshwater pearls, sagged more than a foot above the ground. It did it again. I retrieved a .22 caliber rifle from the cabin. The bird was still there when I returned. Doylanne joined me to watch the bird. It made a *wa wa wa wa wa* sound, and three more birds walked into view. They looked at us and froze like street performers, locking in place for several seconds before pecking at the ground. The jumping grouse sounded again and they froze again, this time looking to the forest. I'd never seen this before. Soon they were back pecking. The first grouse was the leader. I went back to messing with the stove while watching the grouse and the trees, the first layer of trees still mostly summer bright, those deeper in the woods darker and filled with eyes. The forest was alive with predators: marten, lynx, and fox among them, and most frightening of all, owls. What an easy meal a spruce grouse must be for an owl. The beautiful grouse, awkward innocents of the forest, stayed in view for nearly an hour before fading into the brush.

Owls frequently perched on limbs and watched us and all the rest of the creatures dashing and landing near the cabin. They began hooting near dark and sometimes kept it going on and on throughout the night. They called one another, exchanging enchanting words. *Hoo hooo hoo hooo* followed moments later with a response. I usually didn't see them unless they flew. Sometimes I heard them in the air within the trees; or maybe I didn't hear them, I felt them. Sometimes they appeared only moments before they disappeared. I saw them more often along the river. They sat on limbs and held their place as I slowed and idled the boat in front of them. Owls, among the most majestic of all birds, were plentiful near the cabin where they seemed to simply lounge.

"Doylanne, want one of these grouse for dinner?"

"No."

9

Owl

We all know beautiful things can hurt us. It's a common plot. The gorgeous black widow eventually bites. Beauty makes us suspicious and probably should, particularly when we're near what looks too good. This incongruity is common in nature. Plants are notorious for appearing to be something they're not. Take as an example the remarkable water hemlock and its umbrella of tiny white flowers. It is the deadliest plant in North America. It lives in wet environs, in cities, along roadsides, and in the wilds. It is sometimes mistaken for other plants in the carrot family. All very pretty. A small amount will rapidly kill.

Owls are pretty, too, and often associated with dread and death. Under the forest canopy, owls *hooo hooo hooo* and patrol the land of the homestead. During the night they dominate the landscape. They swoop under the branches through an opening and disappear into the branches at the end of the clearing. They sit and hunt small animals. They can easily dispatch a rabbit. When owls are about, all small creatures on the forest floor are in extreme danger.

A troubling attribute of thc owl is they must enjoy killing and eating what they kill. They swallow their prey whole, then regurgitate and spit out the bones and feathers and fur. If it's too large, they rip their victim apart to find the size of morsel they like. Owls are efficient hunters, the killer raptors of the lower trees. Their wing span can be near five feet, and they can weigh nearly four pounds. Muscle, speed, and guts with the capacity to lift three times their body weight.

They hunt by perching on limbs and poles, blending into the gray bark and branches of the spruce and the dying moss. From these stands they plunge silently and clutch their prey. An owl's talons penetrate and kill quickly. They also hunt from the ground where they pounce upon small animals, or from the water where they stand in the shallows, grabbing frogs, fish, and birds.

All this makes owls disturbing creatures. When the owl hooos, we stop and listen. They are the birds of death. Large animals, like the moose, of course, have nothing to fear from the owl, but who knows. Moose might listen for owls too.

Years ago, I read Margaret Craven's *I Heard an Owl Call My Name*. The protagonist in the story, Mark, is dying but doesn't know it. He is sent by the bishop to work as a vicar in a British Columbia village. He grows to love the village and its people, and it is there an owl calls his name. He tells someone and they tell him he will soon die. And he does. I have long associated owls with bad news.

Both great horned and great gray owls, among the largest in the world, live here. The great horned owl, the one I usually see, hunts other raptors too, such as eagles, osprey, and hawks, according to wildlife biologists. Their talons open to a width of up to eight inches and close with the strength of a large dog's bite. The mostly gray great horned owl has horns and a devilish look.

Great grays are gray as well, of course. Larger than great horned and without the tufts, they are also seen along the river but farther from the cabin. They fly with the river. I've followed them in my boat a considerable distance. I expected the speeding owls, with wings as wide as a double bed, to veer and rise over the trees, but they let me follow, probably enticing me to use my fuel. A great gray's flat face in flight is striking and creepy. Eventually, they bend away into an opening in the trees.

When the big owls watch from a limb, their yellow eyes staring, I suspect they consider me as a meal. People have likely faced such a possibility before: An owl attacked a man on a morning run in Salem, Oregon, in 2015; like being hit with a two-by-four, he said. The first contact broke skin on his head. He took off sprinting and screaming and was attacked again, according to a report in the local newspaper. He looked up and saw a large winged animal. A biology professor and animal behavior specialist said it was likely an owl, possibly a great horned owl. Other people have reported attacks as well.

I finished with the stove and turned my attention to wiping the rifle when the grouse returned. Three of them waddled yards from me on the trail to the boat. I placed the open sights on a male with a red slash above its eye. It didn't mind me being there at all. Its head and nap feathers were speckled with white, its covert feathers gray and black rimmed in white, and most spectacular were its greater coverts on its side, long straight gray feathers banded with white tips. I clicked off the safety, and they froze looking ahead to my right. An owl most certainly watched. This grouse pecking grains of sand from my walkway was likely his dinner. They went back to pecking. I reset the safety and laid the rifle across my lap.

"Doylanne, there's an Aesop fable about an owl. A wise owl was awakened by a singing and overly joyous grasshopper. The owl came to the hole in the tree and angrily told the grasshopper to be quiet. The grasshopper sang louder, saying he had every right to do so. The wise owl knew it did no good to argue, so instead he praised the grasshopper and told it how beautiful its voice was. The grasshopper was pleased. The owl invited the grasshopper up to the hole in the tree for a drink, and the grasshopper hopped there and was immediately eaten by the owl."

"Figures," she said.

10

Wilderness Sounds

The shed moved up the to-do list like steam in a kettle, or perhaps a better comparison, grew like the knot in my left hand down from my little finger—some old man growth about a nickel in circumference I tried to rub away every morning. The shed lingered, grew in importance, crouching and waiting, but I wanted to go back under the trees, hike deeper into the woods, chase moose and marvel at hawks, not saw boards.

The best way to compensate for doing something wrong is to do it again and hope for a different outcome. Or maybe I'm confused. Later that day, after the grouse moved on, when the sky resembled pink columbines, I again hiked to the end of King Beaver Pond but continued on south rather than turn right toward the ridge, picking my way inside the willows and highbush cranberries, following the river for a half mile where I came to a stream too wide to step across. I backed up to create a runway, dashed and jumped. I made it with plenty of room, but tripped, a boot caught in a rose bush. I laid for several moments glad no one saw my gracelessness. I kept on along the river under tall spruce and patches of birch. A woodpecker was sounding off nearby, and squirrels stood guard the entire way. I had a destination in mind: a meadow I'd been to many times and a perfect place for a moose, although I'd never seen one there. The undergrowth beneath the white spruce, flowers, berries, and fallen limbs had faded with fall, making easy walking. I set frequently, keeping an eye on the flashes of river. I wasn't getting lost this time. I came to a huge white spruce—clearly dead—so I made a mental note to run up with the boat for boards. I stood among giant trees, their trunks swollen to near two feet in diameter. I kept on and came to a dense patch of willows blocking my way, signaling a meadow ahead. I stopped and considered my route: push through or walk to the river and hike around the jumble of boughs. Going forward meant weaving my way through the tangles. I stepped into the willows, catching my rifle on a branch. I took the rifle off my shoulder and carried it in my right hand, bending over and picking my way. I smelled a skunk. I dropped to one knee and checked the rifle. One shot in the chamber, two in the magazine, safety on. Skunks don't live in Alaska. A mosquito buzzed near my right ear. What did I smell?

Our senses diminish as we age. Sight deteriorates; we adjust our glasses and frequently joke about it, holding our reading material an arm's length away. Taste becomes faded and dull, and we begin liking spicy foods that don't like us. Our sense of smell dramatically worsens, so we miss a lot of smells, and touch is blunted. Our skin toughens and our damaged nerves mislead, and millions of people lose their hearing. We all know this, don't we?

I often hear the surprising sound of the earth humming. Scientists don't know why the earth hums. Maybe the sound comes from the oceans, maybe plate tectonics, maybe the earth's surface like a balloon stretched to near bursting. Regardless, it can be heard around the world. In interior Alaska, at least near our place, the earth is remarkably noisy. I first noticed the earth's hum on a solo trip in the 1980s. I kept turning downriver thinking I was hearing an outboard motor. No. Maybe the accumulated sound of mosquitoes. Probably not. I always hear it now unless it's drowned out by other wilderness sounds. I once thought I heard the hum in a large cathedral in England but was fooled by whispering voices.

Eolian sounds, the noises made by the wind, will drown-out the hum. Sounds of fluttering leaves, scraping branches, bending trees, howls, and whistles bursting like cymbals fill most days. The wind from the east is always a gust, plowing into the trees, pushing the tree tops to one o'clock. Doylanne and I turn our heads and follow until stopped by the image of Denali as the swoosh escapes westward. Only a few blasts and the wind changes course. A north wind blows over us, as the cabin sits low against trees facing the south. The sound grows, building to a crescendo before roaring through the leaves overhead. The most delightful is the wind from the south. Frequent puffs to augment a steady breeze, causing fluttering leaves, bowing willows, and water sparkles.

Seldom is the wind dead, but when it is, the forest fills with the sounds of the river, insects, and animals. The river bubbles and gurgles. Grayling break the surface. Sweepers, pulled under by the current, spring with a swoosh. Heavy rain on the river sounds like drops pounding the hood of a car or a squirrel prancing on the cabin deck.

Animal sounds stop us, startle us. A woodpecker plays a bass drum. It also bounces on the snare at times. When the woodpecker's thumping emanates deep in the woods, the sound is a commanding deep, low reverberation. I count the pecks. I think twelve per musical passage. Over the river, the woodpecker's sound could be a street drummer on a plastic tub.

Swans honk and slap wings. In May they are often in small groups of four or five and can be among dozens on small lakes near the river. In September a particularly noisy ritual occurs when a pair of swans drives away a grown cygnet by honking and thrashing water. Add to the mix smacking beaver tails, quacking ducks, rattling cranes, mooing moose, trilling robins, chattering squirrels, howling wolves, screeching gray jays, moaning porcupines, and ever-present insects—the landscape never lies silent.

During those quiet moments, particularly when the wind calms to a light brush on the face, insects appear. Insects dominate the scene. Peel the bark from a rotting tree and dozens of ants run away. I've never heard an individual ant, but maybe I do hear an ant choir, particularly the combined voices of millions of them. Often insects blaze in my ear. Horseflies sound like floatplanes, spruce beetles like helicopters, bumble bees like chainsaws. But the most ubiquitous and most alarming is the mosquito with its satin wings. The mosquito buzz can wake you from a deep sleep. It weighs about three milligrams, but a sweep over an ear can involuntarily force a hand to fly through the air. The combined power of sounds from the wind, animals, insects, and the river makes the wilderness near our place surprisingly noisy. Peaceful, yes. Silent, no.

How do we hear? You may already know this. A moose pops its antlers against a tree and the disturbance caused by the collision of antler against tree creates a wave through the air (and other mediums such as water). The wave moves away from the tree, growing smaller as it travels away. The vibrations caused by the wave pass through the middle ear to the inner ear. The inner ear resembles a snail and is filled with hairs with little tops waving like russet grass in a meadow. Here the vibrations are converted to signals sent to the brain. Hairs exposed to waves too strong can be irreparably damaged. In the woods there are not many loud sounds. A woodpecker, a scurrying squirrel, or falling branch create gentle waves and soft sounds.

Of all the sounds, though, the river is the most astonishing. Composer Annea Lockwood recorded rivers for decades. "I've always thought of rivers as alive, as live phenomena," she said. Most certainly, we are moved by the aliveness of rivers. The flowing water interacts with all it touches. Lockwood said, "It became very clear to me that rivers create their sound by the way they interact with the materials in their banks through friction." Yes, friction is constant, sometimes violent on a rushing river but also gentle like on rivers such as ours, at least most of the year. Our river is quiet. It allows space for the other sounds of the forest. From the cabin yard, we can hear the gentle plop of rising grayling, the slap of swans' wings, the bang of driftwood against the hull of the aluminum boat, the slap of a beaver's tail, and sometimes the ponderous steps of a moose crossing the river.

Annea Lockwood is right. Rivers create their sound by the way they interact with the materials in their banks through friction.

Our ears are always open, even when our eyes are closed.

When I close my eyes to focus on the sounds, I hear as well as see. With eyes closed, I can see the mosquito heading my way and that's the dreadful way it is.

11

Other Senses

My sight improves in the wilderness because I see more—sounds so pretentious—but I believe it does happen. Relationships become obvious because I witness the natural, unscripted interactions. A mother duck leading her duckling out onto the river is both beautiful and frightening. Why would she do that? Doesn't she know better? On a curve upriver lives a bald eagle. Two ospreys reside one turn downriver. The ability to see the linkages of our actions and the actions of others is enhanced in the woods.

How do we see? When we see a squirrel on a tree branch, light has reflected from the squirrel to our cornea, which is the window to the eye. Our eyes are curved, which creates an upside-down image the brain will eventually turn right side up. The retina does all the complex work of converting light to signals the brain can comprehend. Humans have decent sight but don't come near the abilities of our neighbors in the woods. Eagles, owls, and lynx have tremendous eyesight. The dragonfly, a beautiful and amazing insect, which in our area grows to five inches or so in length, has superb vision. Dragonflies can detect movement much faster than humans.

Not all animals, of course, have good vision. The moose, the largest of all animals in North America, doesn't see well; a bear's eyesight is likely just average.

One night a rattle of gear stored near the cabin woke us.

We ran to a window and there stood three hundred fifty or so pounds of black fur. A bear came to visit.

"The handgun is on the table," Doylanne said. She grabbed the camera. "The rifle's loaded, right?"

The bear looked confused, sleepy like we were. It yawned. I'd read they do that when they're nervous. It didn't seem worried, though it moved away from the cabin and circled. We ran to another window. Hair stood on the bear's back. Its round ears pointed at us. I'd killed a few bears, and this one looked big for around here. It put its paw on the spruce like it might climb the tree. Black bears have non-retractable claws and climbing's natural, but it dropped to all fours and walked toward the back of the cabin. We moved to another window. I shined the flashlight on the bear, and it responded by charging the window.

Bears can run faster than the fastest man. Usain Bolt has run about twenty-eight miles per hour. A black bear runs about thirty, and grizzlies are even faster. A black bear can run a forty-yard dash in under three seconds. A three-hundred-pound athlete running as fast as a bear would be an NFL sensation. I grabbed the rifle and laid it on the bed closer to me. The bear didn't know it, but whether it lived was up to it. I didn't want to kill the bear, but if it didn't leave, I would.

"Anything out there for it to eat?" I asked Doylanne.

"Don't know."

I couldn't think of anything. If it didn't eat something, it'd probably move on. It circled the cabin but didn't hop back on the deck again. It yawned again, maybe a good sign. We yelled at the stinky bear, and it blended away into the dark.

Smell guides like sight. Odors are molecules in the air. Receptors recognize specific molecules. If we don't have a receptor to recognize a specific molecule, we don't smell it. Humans have nearly three hundred fifty olfactory receptors capable of sensing about ten thousand smells, scientists say. Other animals have many more. Bears have the best nose in the world. Scientists say they can smell twenty-one hundred times better than humans.

The dominant smells come from the river, the rain, and plant life. The river smells like rich soil to me, certainly diluted, but still the basic earthy smell of clean soil, the smell gardeners love. It'll emit an oily, musky, even fishy smell. To me this is most evident when the water has dropped to low midsummer levels. The rain is seasoning to all the life in the wilderness, enhancing the smells of the river, but also of spruce, cranberries, bluebell leaves, whatever it touches. We all love the scent after a rain. Doylanne says it's the finest fragrance in nature.

We love the cold of rain too. We're warned about it. We need to exhibit enough common sense to stay out of it, we're told, but once we step out and the drops make their mark, we're okay after all and begin to enjoy it. Usually. There are times it's too cold, and good sense should keep us inside. Rain is special, and we can all experience it no matter where we are, of course. The rain provides us a cold way, and usually harmless way, to connect with nature.

A frequent outing for us is the search for edible natural foods. We're far from experts, so I won't give any advice, but we do favor blue bell leaves, willow leaves, and highbush cranberry flowers; the leaves are put in soups and salads, the flowers in pancakes. I'll have grayling and pancakes at least once a week. For grayling, I heavily salt and pepper the inside and fry it, turning it once. I want the meat moist but done enough to pull easily from the back and rib bones. When on the plate, I pull away the skin and dip the bites in melted butter. It's exceptional. In the fall, I may kill a spruce grouse to add to a dinner, barbecuing it on a birch-fired grill. There's also, of course, the big mammals: bear and moose. Spring black bear is outstanding meat, and moose is the finest meal on the planet. Highbush cranberries make an amazing meat sauce. In the early years, I might have described the food at the cabin as camping food—dried, canned, fare for getting by—but not now. Twenty years ago, the water seriously low and the boat frequently stuck, my sons and I hauled a propane gas range to the cabin. Now our meals belong at the finest restaurants.

How do we taste things? Like smell, taste is reliant on the reception of molecules. The organ most responsible for our ability to taste is the taste bud. On the tongue there are bumps called papilla. Inside these bumps are taste cells. These buds have the ability to differentiate five tastes: salty, sour, sweet, bitter, and umami, a meaty, brothy taste.

Here are two common tastes found near the cabin: spruce and bugs. Working with wood and traveling through the forest results in spruce pitch finding its way to your taste buds. The soft pitch clings to fingers. To me, the taste is not so good, but it is distinctive. Years ago, pitch was sold as spruce gum and was big business. Not surprising, spruce pitch tastes like spruce. Another common taste is whatever is in your mouth after gagging and spitting out a flying bug, usually a mosquito. If your mouth is open, it'll happen. It feels strange too.

How do we feel? Stings, pricks, and pokes go hand in hand with a walk through the woods. The bottom layer of the skin is called the dermis, where touch originates. The dermis has tiny nerve endings transmitting information to the brain about what the skin has touched. Nerve endings detect hot, cold, and in-between, and all the other stimuli, and convert those messages. Covering up is a good idea, but prickly points find their way. Early in a cabin trip my hands are soft. For a week or so they are swollen and ache before they strengthen and toughen. The transformation of my hands is a favorite outcome of a trip to the woods. By week three, my hands become almost impervious to mosquitoes. They land and feast, and I finally notice them when they've had their full. Sounds painful, but it's not. It's all remarkable: the river in the shallows on a hot day, a cool breeze when it's hot, a warm breeze when it's cool, the brush of horsetail against the shins while searching for willow or blue bell leaves to add to the potato soup or spruce tips for tea.

We are reliant on what we see, smell, taste, touch, and hear in the woods, a problem for those with impaired senses, like me.

12

Shed

I didn't know what caused the skunk smell in the thicket of willows but I knew it wasn't a skunk. A bear can smell like a skunk. I turned a tight circle peering into the thicket. Could be a bear. Could be a fox. Could be a beaver. Could be a wolf. I had no idea, but I didn't want to smell it. I hustled out of the willows, turning frequently to see if anything followed me until I broke out onto the river bank and walked upstream where the brush cleared. I emerged in another stand of spruce with decent visibility and continued on to the meadow of waist-high reed grass. I sat against a white spruce and let the sweat dry and the tingling running the length of my right leg fade.

I spent an hour glassing the meadow, but I wasn't thinking about moose. The shed, the shed—we needed one and Doylanne wanted one. We'd been living without a suitable shed for decades. We'd built a small guest cabin years before and used it as the place to put stuff, but we needed more, and needed it now more than ever, its linkage to our goal of making things easier irrefutably linked.

My eighth-grade teacher, in a little school near the Oregon coast, had a sign on the classroom wall: "Procrastination is the waste of time." Next to the sign hung a paddle. He was known to use the paddle. Do it and quit thinking, I told myself—essentially what he used to say. And besides, who doesn't love a shed?

Sheds have a long, long history. From a dictionary: *a shed is a building for storage, temporary shelter (late 15c., shadde), possibly a dialectal variant of a specialized use of shade (n.). Originally of the barest sort of shelter. Or from Middle English schudde (shud) a shed, hut.*

In the Bible, shed is frequently used as a verb, but a variant, "hut," is found in several places as a noun: "The daughter of Zion is left abandoned, like a booth in a vineyard, like a hut in a cucumber field, or like a city under siege" (ISV, Isaiah 1:8).

Cavemen built sheds too. Archaeologist Panagiotis Karkanas concluded cave dwellers in the Kouveleiki caves, near Peloponnese, Greece, had caves used as sheds for tools and livestock.

In England the wealthy built extravagant buildings as yard ornaments. Called English follies, it's not too long a stretch to call them sheds. They are outbuildings removed from the main dwelling sometimes containing the overflow from the main house, i.e., junk—like a shed.

What's a garage if not a shed?

The connex, a large metal container used to haul and store all manner of stuff, is a shed.

And finally, the Nativity scene. Where was Christ born? Certainly, a shed.

A shed means peace too: a shed is a place for everything, everything in its place. I have a place for mine and you have a place for yours. We would never worry about our things if everyone had a shed. We might all get along.

I'd build a shed. Done. Mind made up.

I walked the river's edge back to the cabin and wondered if we'd see anyone else this month. Hunting season excites the adventurers so it was a possibility. Some years yes, some no. It's an expensive long-haul to get to the foothills when the moose trample somewhere else.

I slept well that night, relieved I'd made the decision to build the shed. I dreamt again about my grandparents: I sat too low in the car to see what was outside, so I stood up on the way to their house in the country. Getting there required a long car ride on gravel roads. Dad pointed out features: where he used to go squirrel hunting, a trail to the Wabash, where the old-folks home was. A one-lane gravel road ran parallel with the Wabash. We passed an outboard repair shop and boat yard. A tunnel of overhanging limbs signaled we were close. In their yard stood a shed. That's all I remembered.

The next morning I walked through our small clearing looking for the family of spruce grouse. I saw two birds at the upriver edge of the clearing near our oddly designed outhouse. One grouse was on the ground in the middle of the pathway, the other perched on a nearby tree limb. I talked with the grouse a while, tried to comfort them, and they hung around for a long time before flying off to a tree a few dozen yards away.

The old outhouse, with a hole less than two feet deep, had a seat four feet above the ground to create a suitable distance. The hole was shallow because it had to be.

Five years earlier, the main cabin sat in a pool of melted permafrost. Our oldest son and I moved it with a chainsaw winch. The water near the cabin was deepest on the river side but was no better than a wet sponge anywhere. I built the cabin in 1989 and by 1992 knew the cabin was in trouble. For twenty-four years, we dealt with the water. I built a narrow bridge made from split spruce logs spanning dry ground to the cabin deck. My dying cabin under the trees one hundred feet from the river, the core of a lifetime dream, built by hand from nearby trees, was doomed if left in the water. When there, my boots clung to the earth and sunk my spirits. So, I jacked it up a little every year. The cabin tilted toward the river, so by lifting a side, I could level the cabin and gain another year at least. I sawed three-foot-long logs to crib the front and back corners. Cribbing involved lifting and placing logs under the foundation. I placed hydraulic jacks at each corner and in the middle of the outside foundation logs, and jacked slowly a couple inches before moving to the next jack until I'd lifted the side two feet. When I lowered the cabin onto the cribs, it usually gained about a foot. I wanted more, but it was all I could get. Where the cabin once was, now filled with boreal forest debris dragged there by Doylanne and me, is where I saw the spruce grouse family.

When I staked the land, my dream was to move my family there to live year round. The staking rules required I build a livable cabin, and the staking instructions established requirements for the foundation for such a cabin. I was to dig holes to at least two feet and sink creosote treated posts. The instructions, unfortunately, were faulty. I hit ice at eighteen inches so placed the treated posts there. Within a few years the ice, exposed and disrupted, melted, making for a very unstable, unsightly, and mosquito infested foundation. I suppose the engineers who wrote the instructions expected if a cabin builder ran into ice, he would know not to place the posts there. Not the case for me. I processed it differently. It must be okay because whoever wrote the instructions would know permafrost is common in interior Alaska. The instructions were, after all, written for a specific location between the Yukon River and Denali.

Finger pointing, whining, and barking are all mistakes and a waste of time, I suppose not unlike procrastination. I should have known better than dig to the ice. Here permafrost is most everywhere, but it's not everywhere. It's sporadic. There is not a thick film of ice uniformly spread beneath the boreal forest floor of interior Alaska. There are patches of ice. I happened to hit a patch. When I rushed to build my cabin, I didn't think about what was below my feet.

Because permafrost haphazardly exists less than two feet below the surface of the land, and with no maps or markers to follow, I don't know where to stand or walk. If I walk enough where there is permafrost, my two hundred and thirty pounds can reshape the earth, wear it away. There's evidence of this damage across my property. The land itself is a deception. It resembles the hardened land of eons, but it reacts like bread dough. Eventually, after miles of treading, the landscape becomes a tray of biscuits. It is clearly not what it seems.

So what's going on with the soil and active layer? Water,

gas, minerals, organic matter, and living organisms make up soil. The texture of the soil is determined by the amount of sand, clay, and silt. The agricultural quality of soil is determined largely by the amount of organic matter. In interior Alaska the soils are young, thin, cold, and poor in nutrients—therefore, essentially sterile. Life below our feet is mostly confined to a narrow film of organic matter, and most living organisms live in a world less than a foot or so in thickness called the active layer. When this fragile realm is disrupted by digging or simply walking, the soil warms and melts the ice below. The land sinks and becomes saturated with water. Almost all the land in the region of the cabin, and all of the vast taiga, the world's largest land biome, is untrammeled, so it appears as it has for ages, but its appearance is deceptive. The ice is in jeopardy, and in turn, the soil and active layer above it.

I grabbed kindling from the woodshed. Doylanne had coffee ready.

"I'm going to build a shed."

"Good."

"As soon as I can. I don't have twenty-four years."

"Twenty-four years?"

"It took me that long to move the cabin."

Procrastination is, indeed, the waste of time.

13

Impeller

We have an amazing capacity to tolerate what eats at us: slight knock under the hood of the car, displaced molding after the wind storm, poor lighting in the kitchen, annoying behavior of a co-worker, fading infrastructure of a nation, sinking cabin. We can put up with a lot and we do. Sometimes putting up with defines who we are.

Trumpeter swans swept by us heading downstream. The first set, a pair, pounded straight at us and rose over the trees. The next group, three adults, ran the river, flying a wide curve, staying in view for minutes.

We sat on the deck with morning coffee, both of us extending limbs, stretching like warm spruce pitch into a worm hole. I pulled my arms over my chest and bent at the waist and stretched my knotted lower back, elongating muscles to relieve sciatica pain. Doylanne didn't reveal her pains but used a reverse choke-hold and lifted her head uncurling like a swan.

First on my list for the day was replacing the water pump on an old two-stroke outboard that quit on me the trip before. The small motor powered a twelve-foot aluminum skiff to use in low water or for an emergency if the big boat engine ever quit.

An outboard's water pump is located in the lower unit and is submersed in the water. It pumps water up to and through a metal jacket around the pistons. The cold water keeps the engine cool. A water pump will last a long time when the outboard is run in clean lake water, like it's made to do, but in shallow rivers, it sucks up sand and tiny pebbles, shredding the rubber impeller and thin metal casing. When a pump fails, overheating rapidly occurs and serious things happen: head gaskets fail, and power heads warp. Without a functional water pump, the engine won't run long.

I once talked with an old man at a boat launch about water pumps, and he told a story: he and a friend were hundreds of miles from town on a creek looking for a moose when the pump quit. He thought he had a replacement kit, but no, couldn't find it. So, after a day of discussing options, he sat on the transom and poured water on the engine to keep it cool while they putted their way home. I stashed it away for future use. He had another story as well: his engine overheated and blew the head gasket miles away on a remote northern river. He replaced the pump, and the engine started but didn't have enough power to get the boat on step with the leaking head. He pulled his motor onto the bank and took the head apart and made a head gasket out of a tin dinner plate.

I had a replacement kit. I just had to get the work done.

"I'm going to change the pump in the outboard stashed under the boat."

"Um. Is your face hurting you?" I glanced over. We all know that silly joke and I wasn't playing along.

"I don't need my face to change a water pump."

"You got a nasty scrape."

"Yea, I did. No, it's not hurting me."

"Well, it's sure hurting me." She raised a brow and smiled. "Want more coffee?" She grabbed my cup and headed into the cabin. She was still unhappy with me.

"Doylanne, bring me a cookie, please. Wish we could figure out how to make ice cream." The swans came by again, honking, and Doylanne came quickly out of the cabin with her camera.

"No ice cream, but here." She handed me a cookie covered with whipped cream made from shaken condensed milk.

"You know what's different about Alaska now than when we moved here? There are more old people here now," I said.

"Yeah, we're two of them."

"Everyone was young. Remember? There was no gray hair."

"What's your plan today?"

"Fix the little outboard under the skiff."

I loved my tiny aluminum skiff, an old Smokercraft made in the 1960s, living its final years turned over near the cabin. I bought it in Anchorage in the 1980s. Lying under it was a late 1980s seven-horse, two-stroke outboard with gas can, fuel hose, oars, and oar locks. Outboards are heavy, even the little ones. I lifted the eighty pounds or so onto a stand.

A two-stroke means the downward cycle and upward cycle of the piston completes all four stages of ignition in the engine. It will intake gas and air, compress it, fire a spark, ignite, and dispel the fumes. In a four-stroke engine these four steps are separated into different cycles and occur during stages of the upward and downward stroke of the piston. So fuel and air intake occur at one stage, compression at another, spark and ignition on the third, and exhaust on the final step.

The engine is housed inside a cowling and is connected to a vertical drive shaft spinning the propeller. When started the engine begins its cycle. The drive shaft spins, and a clutch engages the shaft to the propeller. When this occurs, the outboard is sending drive to the boat and moving it forward. The force of this transfer is absorbed by the water around the boat and the transom. What distinguishes outboards from other engines is they are usually cooled by water flushed through the engine from the source itself, in my case a river. Since outboards don't have radiators, this is a necessary part of their design and operation. Almost all of the exhaust of a sterndrive motor is expelled through the lower unit. This is why there are bubbles coming up from the propellers when the boat is started. Water cycles around the engine block and is forced out with the exhaust.

"We could make ice cream out here, you know."

"Let's do, Doylanne. Did you know ice cream is partially responsible for the advancement of the outboard motor? It's a sweet story. Ole Evinrude and his fiancé, Bess, were picnicking on a hot August Wisconsin day on a lake near Milwaukee when Bess said she wished she had an ice cream cone. So, Ole jumped in his row boat and rowed the length of the lake to an ice cream shop. Unfortunately, the ice cream melted before he could get back to Bess, making him mad, so he vowed to build a motor to put on the back of a row boat so this never happened again. He did. He developed the submersed water pump."

"Good story. Read it somewhere?"

"Yeah."

"Ole sounds like a nice guy."

"Girls like guys with boats."

Through the years I've changed a couple dozen water pumps, many times in river sand, usually while engulfed in throngs of mosquitoes,

A memorable water pump adventure occurred the May before when, for some reason, I tried to put one together backward until I broke it. The pump began showing signs of failing on the one hundred fifteen horsepower four-stroke during the trip in to the cabin. At the back of the cowling, a hose, placed so the operator can look back and see whether or not the pump is working properly, expels water from the water jacket. Water dribbled from the hose instead of exuding a strong stream expected with an effective pump. I pulled to a beach and considered camping and changing the pump, but we were on the upper river, within a couple hours of the cabin. I kept going, and we made it. The next day I found a beach near the cabin where I could replace the lower unit.

I'd started carrying an extra lower unit a few years before so I didn't need to go through the work of changing the water pump there in the sand. All I needed to do was exchange the entire lower unit and six bolts, with a little wrangling, only taking thirty minutes or so.

We ran back to the cabin, and I placed the damaged lower unit on my work stand. I pulled it apart, and pulverized rubber impeller bits fell to my feet. I tried to replace the water pump backward, and it's frankly bothered me since. At the top of the water pump casing is the drive shaft and a hole for exhaust. The exhaust hole is in front of the shaft. It's the only possible way for the lower unit to fit with the engine. I had replaced lots of these, as I've said, but on this day tried to install it backward. It didn't fit, but it was close, so I kept trying.

No hurry, I kept telling myself, but I grew frustrated, so took a break on the deck.

"Water pump isn't going on right," I told Doylanne.

"Does it come with directions?"

"Not funny."

"I wasn't trying to be."

Back at the work stand, I applied pressure with old man strength to make the water pump casing fit. I heard a snap. The thick plastic casing now had a crack along one side. A mistake, could have been a big one, but I found a spare casing in my pile of parts. Back again at the lower unit, I immediately saw the problem. I turned the casing around and bolted it in place. I'd tried every way, but I was looking backward.

14

Decisions

The breeze scattered insects while I misread river crossings, messed up the fuel mixture for my chainsaw, failed to tighten the propane line, poured gasoline on a fire, shot myself in a foot. I imagined everything going wrong. We again sat on the deck. I didn't feel so good.

"You've been working hard. How's your back?"

"Sore. I think that's why people hate each other."

"A sore back?" She didn't hear what I was thinking.

"No, we deny the obvious." We drank tea and swatted mosquitoes. "Or maybe it's we don't see what's right in front of us because it's not what we want to see." Doylanne gave me that are-we-going-there-again look I sometimes get. "When we fail to see, we make crappy decisions."

"Would you like sugar?" She held a small dish and a spoon.

"Looks like salt?"

I got a different look.

Decision making doesn't get better with age. It certainly hasn't for me. Apparently, older people find it hard to make decisions, particularly fast decisions. If we must decide on the spot, we're not as able as, let's say, a thirty-year-old (I think of changing lanes on a busy highway at high speeds), but if we have time to consider, we hold our own. Thomas Armstrong describes this reality in his book *The Human Odyssey*: "As an illustration, the mean age for world chess champions—who have three minutes to make a move—is thirty, while the mean age for the 'chess by mail world' champions—who have three days to deliberate—is forty-six."

A decision we consider every trip is what do we do if we break down and can't get the motor fixed. We can't drift home. We navigate four rivers. Since we moved to a larger boat more than a decade ago, a second motor is not feasible. A motor large enough to push the boat takes up too much room and is impossible for me to pick up and move around. A small motor is impractical because it can't adequately push the boat upstream (I've tried). We settled on the solution to carry a spare lower unit, where the water pump is housed and the source of most problems. As I've said, changing the lower unit only requires removing a few bolts, sometimes not as easy as it sounds, though.

It can be hard to get the boat to a good place on the river to do the work. The downstream side of a long beach is usually okay. I anchor the bow with enough slack in the line to pull the aft as near the dry sand as possible and anchor there as well. While standing in a couple feet of water, I exchange lower units. The most difficult part of this job is having enough sustained strength to hold the lower unit in place to start the bolts. I hold the part—weighs about sixty pounds—between my legs, position the drive shaft in the engine head, align the bolt holes, and start the first bolts while leaning over, shifting my feet in the sand and adjusting to the river current. I need to change the water pump after about seven hundred miles of running or one and one-half trips.

Doylanne poured a couple gulps of beer in a dish to catch insects.

"Let's run upriver and get top soil. I dug potatoes today. We should add soil. Can you fix the little old motor later?"

Great idea. The sky turned golden and for a couple miles I cruised on step, slowing at the river stretch below a tall spruce and an eagle's nest. One was home. A bald eagle stood erect on a limb below its nest. The nest, at least five feet in diameter and as many feet deep, rose from the top of one of the tallest white spruce along the stretch. In May there were two eagles, now only one, but the other could be off hunting, we figured.

I pulled to the opposite bank and tied off to a willow to wait.

"It remembers us." Doylanne said.

"I wonder."

The bald eagle is the emblem that almost wasn't. Benjamin Franklin thought the wild turkey to be more worthy. In 1782 the bald eagle was selected as the emblem for the new country despite Franklin's objection. Few images are as uplifting and inspiring as a soaring eagle. We waited for the eagle to show up. Waiting in the wilderness is one my most favorites things to do.

An old friend came to mind. When a kid, I spent a good part of the summer for several years with a friend about twenty miles up the Alsea River on the central Oregon coast. His parents gave me a job for the summer helping out around their little farm and their logging operation. Farming meant milking a cow and hauling hay. Logging meant helping his dad unload his truck and clean things, not actually logging. In the evenings, work completed, we all went to the river and were joined by neighbors for a dinner-picnic. There was always a campfire with joyous voices along one of the most beautiful rivers on earth. We kids played in the river and hunted crayfish, and the adults circled around the campfire and talked.

One summer evening, July 20, 1969, we all listened to the first manned landing on the moon. Four days before, Apollo 11 was launched from the Kennedy Space Center in Florida. We've all seen these launches: the rocket blasts into the sky, disappearing into the heavens. Apollo 11 traveled three days with its crew of Neil Armstrong, Buzz Aldrin, and Michael Collins. When it neared the moon, Armstrong and Aldrin flew the lunar craft *Eagle* to the Sea of Tranquility and landed on the surface of the moon. Collins stayed on the command module *Columbia*. After making it happen and collecting rocks, the *Eagle* launched from the moon and reunited with the *Columbia*. The *Eagle* jettisoned into space, successfully splashing in the Pacific Ocean. Still the highest soaring eagle.

The people making a living and a life along the Alsea River were amazing. Sadly, my friend was killed in a logging accident a few years later.

The eagle never showed up, so we headed upstream. We knew where to go for soil. We zipped by to a stretch of river where the bank allowed easy access to an undercut. With a shovel, I scooped enough soil to fill two five-gallon buckets, all the soil she wanted. We drifted back. Although it didn't take much shoveling, electricity still trickled down my right thigh.

The lone eagle sat still as we putted by. We hadn't seen this behavior, but eagles act crazy together. They're notorious for their death spiral mating ritual. They fly to a high altitude, lock talons, and spiral and tumble toward earth, unlocking just before it's too late. They chase one another in the sky, but before the actually mating, they are calm and can be seen sitting together on the edge of the nest in an eagle snuggle. Partners, they work together building their high-rise apartments with spectacular views.

15

Moon

There's a good reason why we eventually talk about our ailments.

Doylanne strained a rose hip stew into a gallon-sized peanut butter jar brought in years before and added water to fill the jar. She mixed in cups of sugar until the juice was too sweet to drink and added two packages of yeast found on the shelf. She added the lid loosely and set the jar in the farthest corner from the stove.

"This'll be interesting," she said.

I hoped it worked. I needed some pain reliever. The bodies of the young-old, those of us between sixty-five and seventy-five—called YOLDS by some—fade like clothing left outside on the line. Our muscle mass decreases along with bone density, arteries harden, and old injuries come back to life. In our sixties, we watch ourselves age daily in the mirror, and in our seventies, we recognize mobility slipping away with each journey on the trail.

Truth is I hurt most of the time. I know I'm doing better than many and am thankful I'm still here to talk about it. Don't most of us in our mid-sixties live with pain? It's rare to survive to the sixties without illnesses or mishaps nagging us for the rest of our lives. I've broken toes and feet, seriously sprained both ankles, torn ligaments in both knees, broken a knee cap, suffered from sciatica pain, broken ribs, had a heart attack, broken a clavicle now wired together, broken fingers, had surgery on a thumb and little finger, had surgery on my left palm, broken my nose a couple times, and experienced frequent headaches beginning at the base of my skull . . . and those are the ailments I don't mind mentioning. Wounds and injuries pile up. I imagine most people have such a list beginning at the toes and moving upward. Doylanne does. My mom and dad and grandpas and grandmas all did. Those sprains and breaks come home to roost and slow us. But we keep on.

Soon I faced the old outboard. I tore it apart, and the black rubber impeller looked like toes at a rainy music festival. I pulled all of it—the heavy plastic casing, the thin metal lining, the impeller, the gasket, and the plate—up and off the drive shaft. On the drive shaft is a small metal wedge called a key designed to align with a notch on the impeller. With the impeller connected to the drive shaft, it will rotate with the shaft resulting in the pump. The key must be aligned with the impeller during installation, a tricky maneuver. I often struggle with this essential step in the installation. The key is about the size of a morning pill, and my fingers are link sausages.

A guitar player with fat fingers. I played guitar in a rock-and-roll band into my late mid-sixties and always envied the players with the long piano fingers. I started learning guitar in my late teens and in my late fifties began playing in front of people. I'm a short step above garage band guitar musicianship, but I pulled off a few dozen shows a year, playing Paige, Hendrix, and Clapton. (I hope they forgive me.) Shouldn't my fingers be dexterous and sensitive? They're not. I've noticed I lose awareness of my grip if I don't concentrate. For example, I can sense the screwdriver in the grip of my fingers, but if my attention sways, I drop the screwdriver.

I dropped the tiny key. Orange, red, yellow, amber, and russet rushed to my cornea as I focused on the ground. The slice of metal disappeared. I froze. There wouldn't be another of those around here.

"Doylanne, come here. Come here!"

I knelt cautiously, looking for a sliver of gray. My eyes darted across the ground over leaves, under leaves.

"I dropped this part that makes it all work. Come here and look."

Seconds later, Doylanne stood beside me with a metal bucket. She lifted leaves and twigs and dropped it all in the bucket. After the third handful, we heard the plink of the key in the bucket. I finished the task and lowered the boat over the ten horsepower with no plans to use it.

Later, we watched the moon clear the trees at nine o'clock. The shine ran through the window at the front of the cabin, lighting a jar filled with kitchen utensils and streaking over a quilt created by a friend. At three in the morning, the moon sat at the end of a long stretch of river. Doylanne stepped out in the cold to shoot from the deck.

I followed to watch. The moon provided the only light, and I appraised the distance we were from the front door of the cabin. The deck, soon to be frosted, nipped my bare feet. Hers were bare too. "I think I'll go to the river's edge," She said.

"Won't be better there. You'll need shoes."

She shot photos but didn't move. I peered into the black surrounding the cabin. If there was ever a place to feel insignificant, we were there.

"You have enough," I said. "Let's go in." We cuddled under the blankets until I heard her fall off to sleep.

In the morning we drank coffee and talked about the journey to the cabin. A trip requires strength and coordination—both, of course, diminishing attributes. I made a list of ways to reduce our reliance on brute strength. Doylanne pitched in ideas.

"Why not change the water pump at home so the boys can help? How about a strong magnct? Maybe we should pump water from the river instead of carrying it. Maybe a shed with a workbench?" Her list went on and on.

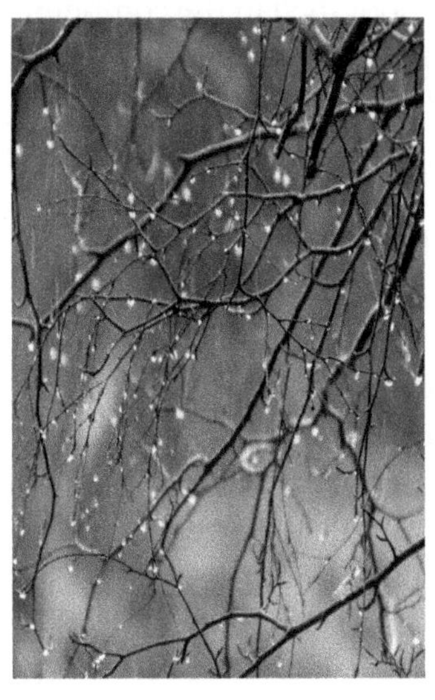

16

Rain Drops

Regret is a big slobbery rain drop. I woke before daylight and watched light change through the back window. Illuminated trees became slow moving figures. Water dropped in sheets from the trees. I noticed the wet, glistening highbush cranberries thick between us and the river. Wild cranberries are a sign of hope. When I walk in the woods in September, cranberries make me happy. The highbush berries shock with tartness, but the sight of them lightens my mood, especially in the rain. Without the red of cranberries, the red bulbs of rose hips, and the pale blue berries sparsely scattered on fields of muskeg, a rainy day in the north woods is too dreary. Bright plants, though, only hold their power for a while. Rain here is different than in town, where I hardly notice it; I don't know where else the contrast is so stark between bright and gray. Here, I watch the sky and wonder when the gray cover will go away. If the air is still, the clouds settle in place and stay a while. With a breeze, they move on. Sometimes, several patches of rain will blow over in a day.

"I think I'll stay in this morning. Maybe read," I said.

I found a map of the river I had looked at hundreds of times and sat back with a cup of coffee. Beyond the river to the south was a drying lake, a half mile or so through white spruce and birch to the edge where a cluster of black spruce and tamarack merged with grasses to the water. I had been to one end looking for a moose years before but not the other end.

"Eric, we should put a full-wall bookshelf in the computer room at home made from spruce boards. Can you saw some when you cut for the shed?"

"Where at?"

"Along the wall where the old organ is."

"Yeah, I'd like a bookshelf," I said, but the future was the opposite direction from where I headed. After all these years, why hadn't I hiked around that lake? What would it look like from the other side? There are dozens of lakes not far from the river, many of them I'd seen, many I hadn't, but this one was so close there was no excuse.

Ask people their regrets, and you'll likely get an answer, maybe a long one since research shows 90 percent of us report having at least one major life regret. Many have more. Regrets are most often related to one of these: romance, family, education, career, or finance. Friedrich Nietzsche said, roughly, we should be happy with the life we've experienced—the good and the bad—because otherwise, things would be different now. Nice, but it's not the outcome for most of us. We regret both what we do and, interestingly, even more so, the things we didn't do. The reason is if we've made a poor decision, we may have time to compensate, but if we don't act, we can't go back and make up the time or recreate the opportunity. I worked for several years as director of an agency serving the aging and disabled. We helped anyone aging or anyone disabled and it turned out to be a lot of people. The staff heard stories of regrets and life's misgivings endlessly. A source of many of my regrets, I think, is I have not looked deep enough at places and thoughtfully answered the mysterious question: where am I now? "These are the days that must happen to you," wrote Walt Whitman in "Song of the Open Road." When we're there, wherever we are, we're there for a reason. We should be present. I haven't always been present.

"The bookshelf will probably take six boards," Doylanne said.

A short time later, I stood on the deck with a cup of coffee and studied a large fallen birch. I could see the outline of the tree through the brush and leaves. After the leaves had dropped in late September, the tree was quite visible and a bit disconcerting. I don't like looking at horizontal trees. I had watched the tree from the distance of the cabin for more than three years.

I walked the short distance with my chainsaw to the birch with the intent to make firewood. It crossed other trees so was off the ground. The root wad at the base stood intact so I went there to make my first cut. There was a hole in the base, the opening about the size of a medium pizza. With a stick I tapped on the trunk. No sounds. I pushed the stick into the opening. The stick hit solid about a foot into the darkness. I probed a little more with the stick before going back to the cabin for a flash light.

"What are you doing?" Doylanne asked.

"Looking in a hole in a tree."

With the light I could see the channel turned downward toward the roots. What is this? I wore work gloves and a raincoat, so I stuck my left hand in the hole and shyly felt my way through the tunnel and around the turn until my arm was swallowed by the tree, my chest and side pressed against the bark. My fingers improvised a minor scale hoping for the recognizable. Nothing. I was in the middle of a decaying tree; lost in a place I'd never been before.

Some critter had a place to hide. I left it alone.

17

Telling Time

I THUMBED THROUGH *Walden,* which I had to do at least once every trip. "Listen to this one: 'Time is but the stream I go a-fishing in. I drink at it; but while I drink, I see the sandy bottom and detect how shallow it is. Its thin current slides away, but eternity remains.'"

Raindrops rhythmically tapped the sheet metal roof. We both sat close to the stove. Doylanne lit candles.

"They used to tell time with candles," I said. "They measured how long it took for a candle to melt, a bit like an hourglass."

"Sounds dangerous."

"We regularly measure time by the movement of substances. Let's see how long it takes to melt an inch of a candle."

"Sounds exciting."

"We regularly measure it—time, I mean. We gauge it by the usage of fuel in the boat, about five gallons an hour; the consumption of fuel in the propane tank, five pounds in twenty days; the collection of graywater at the sink, five gallons in two days; the amount of water hauled from the river, five gallons a day."

"It takes ten minutes to make our morning drip coffee. A minute per cup," Doylanne said.

"We pee every 2.4 hours."

"Depends on the cups of coffee."

"I can tell time by jobs too," I said.

A whole life of jobs. I sat there by the stove and carved up thirty years of work into neat five- to ten-year segments, each with its own location, routine, and predictable outcome.

Whenever I changed jobs, I'd figure out the fastest or most enjoyable route to drive. I worked in Palmer or Wasilla, Alaska, and our home was ten miles or so from the two small cities. To get to work, I drove the same route daily. This is rural country with mostly blue asphalt roads, and through the years new roads would join the roads I traveled. I watched those new construction efforts but never paused long enough to investigate. Recently, since retirement, I started driving where I'd never been before, and I learned more about my community. Back in the woods are thousands of people I didn't know were my neighbors. Subdivisions with dozens of homes had sprung up through the years. I turn around at gated communities. I didn't know walled communities existed near my home. I discovered I didn't know the place where I was living.

Several years ago I attended a work conference in Los Angeles, the meeting at a hotel near the airport. On a warm afternoon after our meeting, I took a bus to Sunset Boulevard—at least that's where I think I was—and walked the thoroughfare for a couple hours, stopping in shops and gawking. I was struck by the beautiful people and the convertibles. I was passing a nail salon in early evening when I heard "Hey, where are you going?" The door was open to the shop, so I stuck my head in to see three women watching me. The one with her hands stretched out in front said, "Do you know where you are?" I smiled and searched for a response. "A bus stops every few minutes across the street. You should go back." I couldn't help but notice how beautiful these smiling women were, but I didn't question why. They were intense. I know that emotion. Maybe a local resident didn't give much thought to the fifth commandment. The pretty smiles said go back.

I didn't know where I was.

Once Doylanne and I were in New Orleans, walking in the French Quarter and heading back to our hotel late after an evening listening to music. Two men stepped from a stairway blocking our way on the sidewalk. "I bet I can tell you where you got your shoes," one of them said.

"What?"

"For two dollars, I bet I can tell you where you got those shoes."

"No, you can't," I said. We all smiled.

"Yeah, for two dollars I can tell you where you got your shoes."

"Okay," I said.

"You got two dollars?" I turned away and pulled the bills from my wallet.

"Right on. You got your shoes on Bourbon Street in New Orleans." He pointed to the street sign. I laughed and handed him the two bucks. "Thanks folks," he said. "You get on to your hotel." He knew more about us than we knew about him. We headed up the street oblivious to the place we walked through.

This place to that place and back again isn't an informed life; it's an existence with blinders. Lots of decisions are influenced by the myopic views we hold because we seldom venture from our daily line. We don't know where we are or who we are, and ultimately, we end with regrets. Perhaps that's why we don't much like one another. How can we like what we don't know? If I don't know about you, why should I ever care about you? If I don't know about the wilderness, why should I care about it. If I don't know about the short lives of the food I eat—plant or animal—why should I give it a second thought? John Steinbeck put it this way in *The Winter of Our Discontent:* "I wonder how many people I've looked at and never seen."

When we visited our son, who attended university in Manhattan, I stood frozen, stunned, looking at the skyscrapers and the structural beasts of a monstrous city. He went from Wasilla High to Uptown. One day he drove country roads, the next walked Gotham's city streets. Doylanne and I went to see what he was seeing. We immediately saw that between John Jay dormitory and the wilderness is a cultural divide difficult to understand. On the streets of New York City, I certainly waddled like a duck out of water. I suspect it is also beyond the ability of many in the city to understand our river in Alaska.

We need bridges.

When I stood on Sunset Boulevard and watched the beautiful people or in Times Square and watched the river of people, I was amazed. When I stand on a wilderness lake's edge watching twenty trumpeter swans paddle among a hundred ducks, I am equally amazed.

When Doylanne and I travel out of Alaska, we go to cities. All of our years have been in rural America, so we both find cities fascinating—the sights, sounds, and concentration of people. Through the years we've wandered through downtown parts of several cities, and we always say, "Let's come here and stay a month," but we haven't yet. We know a place can't be known in few days. Perhaps a few weeks would give us a good start.

Here are simple questions for city residents: Do you store large amounts of food? Use a freezer with months of meat and other perishable food? Do you have a car? What's it like to live in an apartment building, maybe with the same neighbors for years? Do you own a gun? Is it kept loaded? How do your children get to school? What is your main public safety concern? How well do you know the demographics of your city? Do you venture from your line? What do you think of rural dwellers like me? I can venture a reasonably educated guess for answers to many of the questions, of course, as we all can, but only a presumption. Drawing conclusions about others is prejudicial and most certainly disrespectful. When Doylanne and I walk through a city, we can't possibly know where we are.

I've considered the extremes so far—wilderness and cities—but what about the vast middle? Small cities and the rural enclaves are the places I know most about because that's where I've lived. Like city life, small-town America is far too complicated to generalize, though it's tempting to try. Generalizing is discourteous.

Perhaps the most ubiquitous of all institutions in America is the public school. I taught in high schools in Oregon and Alaska and spent more than a decade as a principal of two elementary schools in southcentral Alaska. That's the landscape where I lived my life, and I have at least, if not always accurate, an authentic perspective about its culture. The school is a good place to look.

My first teaching job was high school English in the foothills of the Cascade Mountains in southern Oregon. I was hired to coach wrestling and teach English. They were confident I knew wrestling and hoped I knew English. Shortly after school began, I was told by the principal to attend a school board meeting to discuss my philosophy of teaching English. A board member requested my attendance because new hires were rare in this small school district where the trout and steelhead fishing was so good. I was twenty-three years old and didn't have a philosophy. So I fretted about this for days leading to the meeting. At the meeting, I said I believed in teaching the basics, and I gave a short lesson on using hyphenated words. The next day the principal said the board loved me. They wanted the basics. The wrestling team was small in numbers, but the young athletes were tough guys. I tried, but I couldn't work them too hard. It was okay to work so hard you puked off the side of the wrestling mat. In the classroom, the kids were noisy but always respectful. The principal would stop by weekly and catch me in the hall and ask, "Eric, you teaching the basics?" Doylanne and I had dinner at his house once a year. I fit this small town like an old shoe. I knew where I was.

But we were broke all the time. My first teaching contract in 1976 was for $9,585, about $700 a month take home. Not enough, so we moved north to Alaska to another small town where the pay was a little better. There I taught English in a school with teachers from across the country, teachers with degrees from Southern Oregon (me) and Harvard. None of us knew this rural region of Alaska where the dominant culture was Yupik. I ventured from my home to school and back. During the summer months, the daily destination was a fishing stream. The locals were friendly and encouraging, but knew I'd be moving on soon. The principal assigned me a drama course to teach, wanted me to direct a play. I chose Thornton Wilder's *Our Town*. The students were polite, fun, and talented. We pulled it off on three boisterous nights in a packed gymnasium. The entire town turned out, and students became stage stars like in every small town. Doylanne and I and our two sons—one born in this town, the birth administered by a doctor who showed up on a snowmachine—moved on after two years. I was comfortable with the school community but didn't reach out to link with the broader culture, one of my regrets. I am like many people: a non-observant traveler on a winding narrow road.

"Eric, it takes an hour to burn an inch of candle."

I measured the diameter of the candle: one inch took an hour to melt.

"Will you set up the bear fence?" Doylanne asked. The rain slowed. On one side of the cabin, I'd built a workbench where I stored hand tools, a freezer powered by a generator and solar panels, and a portable washing machine powered likewise, all of it a reminder we needed a new shed. I'd put an electric bear fence around the area during our trip in May, and it worked. We heard the bear near daylight and watched it slide between the two strands of the wire fence (Note: This is not an endorsement or directions on how to use a bear fence. I didn't follow the directions anyway). Once inside the small enclosure it sniffed around and pawed the freezer. Its nose hit a wire strand. It bolted into the brush.

Black bears *(Ursus americanus)*, sometimes mistakenly taken less seriously than their cousins, the grizzly and polar bear, thrive around our cabin. In the spring and early summer, they can be everywhere: in the yard, in the river, or looking in a window from the cabin deck. They move away from the cabin by July, although they are occasionally seen. By late summer bears have moved to the berry patches. Knee-high blueberries are on hillsides and ground-level blueberries are inches above the surface in open expanses of meadow. Lowbush cranberry patches are commonly thick in forested areas near the river. In the winter, black bears hibernate in dens in the forest.

Remembering the bear squeezing between the two strands of wire in May, I installed three strands and watched the woods. I now sometimes think too much about bears, something I didn't use to do. I would sleep outside anywhere. Now I've read too many bear stories and have taken too many trips to the woods. Now in a tent on a beach in central interior Alaska, I lie awake late and have weird dreams.

At the cabin we keep a clean camp so bears aren't encouraged to visit. We don't have a dump. We haul garbage hundreds of miles to town because we want bears to move along. If one enters our yard, we want it to quickly pass on by and not give us a second thought. Most of the time, a bear will jump on the deck, sniff the shed, and amble off to the woods. That's what I want it to do. If it doesn't, I have to do something about it, a messy business I don't want to think about.

I know more now, I suppose, about the mile behind my cabin than the mile behind my house in town. I love my cabin, and the wilderness where it sits, but I regret I've failed to learn more about other places. The more I know about my surroundings and my animal neighbors—two- and four-legged—the more capable I may be as I age, in the woods as well as in town. Where I am now is more important than ever.

In the dark from our bed, I watched a red moon through the back window and imagined flames, sparks, and falling ashes from Mount Doom near Mordor, the display confined to a thin line of light. Beyond the line all was black except eyes in the trees.

"Something's always watching out here. Tomorrow I'm hiking to the end of the lake across the river," I said.

"Too far to shoot a moose, Eric"

"I'll just look."

18

Frost

I WOKE NOT SURE WHERE I was. Cold morning. Our fire went out in the night.

"Doylanne, you awake?"

"Yes."

We sprung up together. I built a fire and Doylanne started coffee. The thermometer outside the front door read twenty-eight degrees, and the season's first frost sparkled on the deck. The sky resembled a broken stoneware flower vase. The water dropped during the night, and a small beach formed on the opposite bank. This river's up-and-down behavior was normal. If the rain poured in the mountains, it could rise in hours. Likewise, growing ice could reduce its flow dramatically.

"Did you hear the cow call in the night?" I asked.

"No, but I heard an animal on the deck. Probably a squirrel. Maybe the mink I saw yesterday." A mink dashed across the yard the day before, and Doylanne wanted a photo. She took her camera to the outhouse, hoping to encounter the mink but captured ice crystals on the window instead.

The cow call north of the cabin sparked my interest. There might be a bull with her. I didn't want to go seriously hunting yet, although I'd already been out looking several times with a rifle, which is pretty serious. I had lots of chores to do before I wanted a moose, besides, freezing a moose for the duration of our trip, about three more weeks, would take a lot of energy. We could use a small freezer powered by a generator and rotate the packages among coolers and the freezer if we had to. Mostly, though, a moose is too much work this early in the trip. I hadn't burned the carbon yet.

Man wasn't made to haul a moose. I looked this up: The average man weighs a little under two hundred pounds, and without prior training, using competitive weightlifting guidelines can bench press 135 pounds, deadlift 155, and squat 125. Doesn't seem impressive to me. A typical adult Alaska bull moose will stand near seven feet at the front shoulder and weigh more than fourteen hundred pounds. A field dressed moose, which is packed out, is in the seven-hundred-fifty-pound range. Occasionally, hunters bone-out the carcass, significantly reducing the weight. After my heart attack, I asked my cardiologist if it was okay to pack moose. He looked at me like I was nuts, smiled, and said, "No, carrying heavy weight on your back is the most difficult thing you can do."

I'd worn down, my back now feather-soft, the discs—pillows between the spine's vertebrae—shrunk and didn't work like cushions anymore. My bones rubbed together. Carrying a moose hurt, so did hauling an outboard, containers of fuel, logs, or buckets of water.

It's mostly back-straining work along the river. Hunting from ATVs doesn't work well in the brushy land where we are, so it's a pack board and sometimes a winch. I can pick up a quarter—one hundred twenty pounds or so—off the ground and set it on the bow, but I can't carry it far enough to be too helpful. So it's good all shots I take are a short distance, most less than one hundred yards. If I don't hike too far off the river, I can do it. It's a hard pack but doable. Hunting moose this way is old school, but it's what I must do to hunt here. I suspect it's the reason I haven't developed shooting skills or kept up with advances in guns, optics, and the technology linking the two in the field. I hardly need binoculars, and my old 30.06 works fine for moose and black bear. A friend of mine and his regular hunting buddy search for moose in an alluring way in this area. They run the rivers until they find a moose. After the kill, they set a tarp lean-to and build a campfire and sleep in the open with the moose hanging nearby. After a day or two, after the work is done, they load the boat and continue on until they fill their tags or must go home. Roughing it is their fun. Moose hunting this way is nearing its end for me and Doylanne, the two of us hunting with a pack board.

"Hunting today?" she asked.

"No. I might look around, though, hike in the woods."

"Sounds like hunting?"

"Or I might read a book, sit on the cabin deck, and watch ducks and beavers paddle to somewhere."

I sat on the deck tossing about the question why. Research reveals a decline in determination as we age but maybe not to the degree many think. Some good news. Sure, work has moved on without us, which might be dismaying to some, but now we have time to volunteer at the recycling center or food bank or wherever our interests lie. There are many stories of old and older people making significant contributions: elders like Nola Ochs who graduated from Fort Hayes State University in 2007 at the age of ninety-five with a degree in general studies; or ironman Lew Hollander, an Oregonian who competed in triathlons in his eighties; or John Glenn who traveled in space at seventy-seven; or Peter Roget who published his famous thesaurus at seventy-three; or Grandma Moses who revealed her first painting at seventy-six. All are astonishing and the list could go on and on. We should be inspired by them.

Sometimes the freedom associated with aging results in new businesses, incredible community commitment, and great creative works. Indeed, many studies have shown that the old with goals and determination, i.e., grit, are less inclined to experience mental and physical impairments and tend to live longer. It's interesting, too, that we don't have to find the holy grail; little goals can have the same positive result as grandiose, change-the-world endeavors.

I whined about stuff too much, but Doylanne was used to it.

Growing up, my dear mom would say jokingly, "You'd

whine if I beat you with a new belt." Woe is me, sciatica moved in to stay, muscle a cold memory, and dreams floating like clouds, out of reach.

"Doylanne, what does sand do in an hourglass? What do you call it? Does it flow, drain, filter? What's the proper description?" She pulled Webster from the spruce board bookshelf and found hourglass: "an instrument for measuring time consisting of a glass vessel having two compartments from the upper of which a quantity of usually sand runs in an hour into the lower one."

"The sand runs. I like runs better than falls or drains."

"There's time, Eric, probably."

"You mean I'm not dead yet?"

"Yes, that's what I mean."

19

Lynx

When I don't do something I said I would, the reel plays on and on and never ends. One of these days I'd better get to it if it's going to get done.

"I'm going to build a shed. I already said so. I just have to get going. I want a space for all your stuff."

"My stuff? Good to hear. We get here; we empty the shed so we can store the things we bring up; we put it all back in the shed again when we leave. We need more storage and a place for our stuff," Doylanne said.

"Isn't most of it yours?"

"No, Eric. It's not. Let's take out those old shoes this time, make some room."

We'd kept old shoes and boots for decades: my shoes, her shoes, our sons' shoes, and the shoes of friends who visited. Oddly, people left their shoes and boots. I fashioned a necklace with them, stringing them along a rope, and hung it inside the shed. We called it the Wall of Shoes. It took up a lot of room. Most annoying, though, squirrels built middens and filled all the shoes with spruce cones, grass, and mushrooms.

"You sure? All of them?"

"All of them."

"It's going to be a pretty day. Let's go for a boat ride before I tackle the shoes. Maybe Yamashita left his treasure in a berry patch."

"Who?"

Departing the cabin, even for a short trip, isn't like

leaving for the store in town. We leave with enough gear and food to camp for a couple days. We also carry a tool set, satellite phone, emergency pack, medical kit, and firearms.

We ran the river an hour, slowing for photos. On one corner, I saw movement in the river. I ran closer for a look. A lynx looked over at us. Sightings of lynx have been rare through the years, although tracks are often seen on beaches. I kept the boat back so not to panic it. It paddled steadily but didn't appear to be in a hurry. Lynx are large, short-haired wild cats, weighing nearly forty pounds with a life expectancy of about a dozen years in the wild. This one looked big with amazing tufts on its ears. It paddled on and I swerved away and ran farther downstream to a small creek entering from the east. Lynx, bears, moose, wolves, eagles, osprey, porcupines, beaver, squirrels, mink, hare, and all of our other neighbors have a purpose—to survive, make it through the hour and the day, find the next meal to stay alive, and perpetuate their species. They likely don't concern themselves with why. This lynx looked for food.

Below a high bank, I tied off the boat, and we walked up to a stand of large spruce where I expected to see cranberries, and they were there. Berries adorned the active layer. On a stump was a rusted three-pound coffee can, a boot string strung through a hole in the bottom. I soaked the string in water. Short pulls are supposed to sound like bull moose, long pulls lovesick cows. Doylanne picked berries and I called moose. An hour later we headed back to the cabin with berries. I talked about the shed.

My plan called for a work bench, room for a bed, and space to park at least two snowmachines under the overhang. I'd use white spruce for the entire structure and cover it with metal roofing. Doylanne said she liked the plan and asked about nails and screws. Obviously, she wanted me to get going on the project, and I think she thought it might be happening and was happy. I could feel her excitement and desire to help.

It may come as a surprise, but older people are happier, according to what researchers say. Sure, there are aches and pains, failing senses, declining mobility, regrets, reduced income, loss of family, friends and social connections, and a fogginess shrouding life's purpose. And despite those obstacles, many older people are happier than they were at earlier stages in their lives. I fit in such a group, as does Doylanne. Could it be we gain some control over our fears?

I like making boards. It makes me happy, but I'd been dragging my feet, and it was time to move forward. I came to sawing boards late in life after hauling boards for years to the cabin. Expensive, heavy boards filled a part of my boat until I'd had enough and decided to do it myself. Where you build what you need, a board is a valuable commodity. On our property, certainly, but also almost everywhere along the rivers, standing dead trees and trees recently fallen laid rotting, so I began learning and practicing. Dead wood surrounded us. White spruce, a light, soft, beautiful wood, looks to be in trouble in the region of Alaska I know. Permafrost is melting and the large trees with shallow roots are dying and collapsing because the soil is changing. It's common to see trees leaning on one another. They're sometimes called drunken trees. Researchers say the trees in the central region are moving westward to the edge of the tundra. The forests have changed over the past thirty years.

If a tree's been on the ground only a year or so, it can still yield beautiful wood. If it's been held off the ground by other trees, it's still harvestable after three years, at least much of it is. A fallen tree's rot seems to expand upward from the truck of the tree. Rot in a standing dead tree often reaches downward from the broken top. When evaluating a tree to harvest, it's a judgment involving amount of work for amount of yield. Most of the time spent salvaging a tree is in the setup. With a sharp chain, the sawing is the fastest and easiest part of the task. I take the sawmill to the tree. Certainly, it's best if the tree is close to the river because I'll eventually carry boards to the boat. I limb the tree and buck it in eight- to twelve-foot lengths. Usually, I winch the logs to a level place. I complete one log and evaluate the boards milled from it before winching the second log. I've wasted lots of time and resources winching logs to a work area and finding the wood too rotten to be useful. Getting the first cut is the trickiest part. I've tried lots of ways, including freehand, but a rail designed for the purpose works best for me. I don't follow the directions exactly, but I usually get a workable first cut. I set the saw to the depth I want and start sawing. I use a monster chainsaw with a twenty-five-inch bar and a ripping tooth chain. When it's sharp enough, the saw will pull itself along and I'll guide. If I find myself pushing, it's time to change chains. A key to a successful day is keeping the chain sharp. Any time spent cleaning the log seems to help.

"I'm going to get one at the corner downstream. I'll see where it falls."

Whenever we're on the river, we point out future trees. We'd had our eyes on a few trees a short way from the cabin.

"Want any help?"

"No, I'll knock it over and look at it."

"Be careful."

I ran the boat downstream to the trees. The top of a sixty-foot standing dead spruce was broken, the limbs and bark gone with the wind. The nearly two-foot-in-diameter base stood about one hundred feet from the river's high-water mark. Its lean made it predictable. I dropped it toward the river. Rot had taken over the top, but it looked like I could easily get four eight-foot logs and more than twenty boards from this tree. These boards could be ripped into two-by-fours, two-by-sixes, and so on, so this tree was worth the effort.

I stood on the bank and could see smoke curling above the cabin roof. With the lazy wind blowing toward her, Doylanne would have heard the chainsaw. If she were on the deck, she'd be able to tell the story from the noises wafting her way.

20

Be Careful

A big shed takes loads of boards and lots of work. Cutting wood has always been hard work and has been a slowly evolving technology, starting I suppose with axes with stone heads, inching along to metal axes, to saws, to motorized saws, hydraulic shears, and lasers. I used a high-end saw, powered by a two-stroke engine emitting the same emissions as an automobile. Chainsaws are remarkably simple and deadly machines. The engine turns a sprocket. The chain resembles a bicycle chain with teeth running on a bar connected to the sprocket. The chain rotates fifty-five to sixty miles per hour.

The monstrous fear for both of us is injury or illness. The daily mantra is "be careful." Many years before, when we lived in Oregon while I attended graduate school, I removed the training wheels from our oldest son's bike. He was practicing on the paved playground at the local elementary school. He beamed, ready to go, and I gave him a little push. He rolled smoothly and turned toward the see-saw, picked up speed at a slight incline, and ran head first into the steel bar serving as the fulcrum. Blood gushed from his nose. I carried him to the car and drove to the hospital. It took weeks of recovery, of packing and unpacking his little nose, to get over his injury. I vowed to be more careful and frequently repeated the bicycle story to myself as a reminder.

Here at the cabin, we're on our own and must be careful.

There are no hospitals. The best we can do is think a few steps ahead. What is the most likely outcome if I do this? The reaction to an action? We look forward as far as we can.

Once, a few years back, I hunted alone under the trees on the edge of a meadow two miles downstream from the cabin. I waited for a moose to show himself. He was there, banging about in a thicket a couple hundred yards away, but he wasn't stepping out of the brush. The sun had dropped below the trees and it would soon be too dark for a shot and too dark to safely run the river. I watched the thicket through binoculars until a blanket was pulled over my head.

I turned on a head lamp, gathered my stuff, and picked my way back to the river bank. Solo departure usually goes like this: step into the boat, start the outboard and accelerate, pushing the bow firmly against the shore, and go on shore and retrieve the anchor. This time I slipped when I stepped back into the boat with the anchor, falling and smashing my chest against the gunwale, my left hand under me. Fortunately, I rolled into the boat. The boat surged ahead and turned into the river. I jumped up and took control. While I putted back to the cabin in the dark, I saw my son at the playground when I promised to be more careful. I could have easily bounced out of the boat. During the few weeks we stayed at the cabin, the ring finger I broke healed, twisting toward my thumb a bit, a further reminder to be more careful.

From the cabin, the only fast transportation is a helicopter, and it's not easy to get a helicopter. Bottom line, and we both know this well, if we get seriously hurt, we are in serious trouble. So we try to be thoughtful: don't get burncd, don't gct cut, don't slip, don't fall in thc watcr. Wc repeat "be careful" constantly.

"I'm running to the boat."

"Be careful."

"Want me to start a fire?"

"Be careful."

"I'll get the milk from the cooler."

"Be careful."

"I'm going to take a shower."

"Be careful."

Running boats, carrying motors, operating chainsaws, climbing ladders, chopping firewood, hiking in the remote woods, and chasing away bears can go wrong in a hurry.

I'd had enough logging and sawing for one day. Worn out. I sat and caught my breath and watched the cabin. A book and stove were sounding good. I fired up the outboard and imagined a sigh. She would be listening for an engine. She'd figure I was on my way home. It's smart to listen carefully and be fearful here, at least a bit.

"Could you hear the saw?"

"Yes, the chainsaw was quite loud. Is the tree okay for boards?"

"Yes, quite good."

"Let's use the walkie-talkies."

"Yeah, tomorrow. I'm going to get the logs off the ground."

"You going to saw boards?"

"Yeah."

"Be careful."

I worry about cuts, falls, and fires, of course, but they're not what I fear the most. Nothing I do at the cabin is more dangerous than driving fifty miles an hour on an icy, curvy two-lane highway, which I do nearly every day in town. We face dangers wherever we live. What I worry most about is forgetting why I spent more than thirty years traveling the rivers to build this little homestead. I fear losing the desire to experience the wilderness. I must, like all of us, transition comfortably from doing to being, as Joan Chittister's describes in *The Gift of Years*. She put it this way: "What am I when I am not what I used to do?" Is there a value to the homestead when I am no longer developing it? Will I be happy being beneath the trees when I can no longer lift the end of a log? Happy old people successfully make that transition.

21

Wolves

The next afternoon Doylanne and I sat on the cabin deck again and listened to wolves. I recorded a session on my phone. I missed my little dog. Gray wolves are the forefathers of all the tall and short, stubby, and angular, dog creatures we have as pets. Yes, domesticated dogs are gray wolves, but they are juvenile wolves never reaching maturity. Temple Grandin calls them wolf puppies. Genetically, domesticated dogs are almost all wolf. They look different as a result of breeding, but there are not significant genetic differences. In her book *Animals in Translation*, Grandin points out that gray wolf pups have blunt noses and floppy ears that turn to upright ears and long pointed noses in adulthood. I've had three toy poodles through the years that resembled puppies when they were puppies and puppies when they were grown. Grandin also points out that dogs with a wolf-like appearance retain more wolf-like behavior. Dogs bred to not look like a wolf, won't much act like a wolf. A toy poodle doesn't act much like a wolf. I suspect neither does a dachshund.

Buck, the dog protagonist in Jack London's *Call of the Wild*, looked like a wolf. Remember the story? He was stolen and taken north and after repeated beatings by vicious men and hardened by miserable living conditions in the brutal north, Buck makes the transition from noble and pampered pet to wolf. London writes: "His development (or retrogression) was rapid. His muscles became hard as iron, and he grew callous to all ordinary pain. He could eat anything, no matter how loathsome or indigestible; and, once eaten, the juices of his stomach extracted the last least particle of nutrient; and his blood carried it to the farthest reaches of his body, building it into the toughest and stoutest of tissues. Sight and scent became remarkably keen, while his hearing developed such acuteness that in his sleep he heard the faintest sound and knew whether it heralded peace or peril."

Buck grew up.

"Doylanne, let's get another dog."

She tilted her head the way that means "No, let's not."

The wolves howled for several minutes, their notes blending to a mesmerizing moan. How does it end for a wolf? Most wolves must die alone, I suppose; they wander off in the woods and die after a fight with a rival pack member or a lost battle with malnutrition or disease.

Some wolves, though, have large followings to the end. They are watched by scientists, fans, and hunters, and their deaths change people and public policy. Wolves are considered quite sociable by wild animal standards. Observers like Adolph Murie and Gordon Haber noticed their family-like characteristics. They can be friendly and playful and heart-beat serious and deadly. Wolves come and go through a pack—like a human family—and they can set up residences for generations—like a human family. Pack members fill roles essential to the success of the pack. Life is difficult after the death of a key family member, such as an alpha male or female. Like human families, wolves teach their young to adapt and cope. Wolf packs can consist of moms and dads and grandmas and grandpas. Wolf researchers point out all these things.

Wolves are symbolic of wilderness, and the death of a wolf can make national news. In Yellowstone, O-Six, an alpha female, became a celebrity. She seduced male members of the Druid pack and was a renowned hunter and alpha female. Wolf watchers followed her movements. Her great-grandmother from western Canada was a wolf released in Yellowstone in the reintroduction of the species in the mid-1990s. In *American Wolf*, Nate Blakeslee describes O-Six: "Her cheeks were also white, and an unbroken streak of white ran from the tip of her head to the end of her nose, tapering off into a buff along the sides of her snout."

She was a beauty, and the dog protagonist in Blakeslee's book. Her death shook up a community and made national news. O-Six certainly didn't die alone.

Near Juneau, a black wolf befriended a community and became a star. In *A Wolf Called Romeo*, Nick Jans recounts his personal experiences with Romeo and how a community came to love a large, social wolf who lived near human activity and interacted dog-like with mankind. I grew to like Romeo while reading Jans's book. But Romeo was bound to get killed by a long rifle shot if all the other ways death comes to a creature in the wild didn't get him first. Romeo didn't die alone. His killer was there with him. Jans's writing brought Romeo's tragic end to national attention.

"We don't need a dog, Eric."

She was right, of course. I could listen, imagine, and marvel at the wolves in the forests near the cabin and not have to feed them or pay vet bills. Wolves could be my imaginary pets I never care for. Maybe I could learn to identify calls like many others have, making me family enough. In London's story, Buck grows closer and closer to the wildness until it is the call of the wild and wolves, those creatures responsible for the call that pulls him away, finally and completely, from mankind. I want to believe Buck didn't die alone. Maybe his wild family provided a dog-like bedside manner when he lived his last hours.

"I wish we had a dog who would run off all the beavers," I said.

"I don't want another dog."

"A dog might run off a bear."

"Um. Or get eaten by one."

"Wolves eat bears and they're dogs."

"Eric."

No dogs for us.

I didn't know wolves killed and ate bears until I read Tom Walker's *Wild Shots.* Walker, a writer and photographer from Denali, Alaska, described this encounter: a pack chased a grizzly with two cubs up a hillside. The momma bear turned repeatedly to fend off the wolves. She would charge at the wolves and retreat farther up the hillside. The cubs wedged behind her at times and other times darted off, making it impossible for the confused and tiring momma bear to respond to all the attacks. The bears and the wolves disappeared in a thicket. Moments later a single cub sprinted from the thicket downhill followed by the mother bear. From *Wild Shots*: "One by one, the wolves wandered out of concealment, some flopping onto the tundra to rest. After a bit, a large white wolf (perhaps the East Fork alpha female) trotted out with a portion of a cub in its jaws and lay down to feed."

"There's a beaver." Doylanne pointed to the river. "Eric, beavers are going to kill all the birch on this river."

Gnawed off birch covered our property like spines on a porcupine's back. Birch stumps, sharpened, pointed, stood about two feet in height. A couple years before, we'd begun protecting trees from beaver attacks by wrapping trunks in aluminum foil and chicken wire: it worked some, but trees were still gnawed down by beavers.

Only two nights before, we'd lost a small birch despite aluminum foil. The tree fell over the path to the outhouse. We were disappointed, but the dead tree was useful as firewood, a task for another day. The next morning the tree was gone, vanished. A beaver must have pulled the tree to the river while we slept. I was fed up with them. Whatever ate beaver in the wild wasn't doing its job well.

"Think I should kill a few of the beavers here?" I asked Doylanne. She nodded. She was tired of seeing dead birch.

The northern forest needs birch. From a distance, an interior Alaska forest is a patchwork of conifers and deciduous trees with birch the most prominent. There is a hillside I've watched for decades that I would describe as a quilt of forest green, lime green, and forest-fire black. Spruce are muted green, birch are lime, and the burnt forest is a shoe-sole brown. Tree scientists study the tops of trees—called crowns—and diagnose health. Recent surveys revealed more than a half million acres of birch trees with thin, discolored unhealthy crowns south of the Yukon River to southcentral Alaska. A beaver gnawing down nature's most beautiful tree in one night—a tree needing decades to grow—didn't seem fair. Not fair at all. I agreed with Doylanne.

Yellow birch leaves color the northern forest crown in September. The country here is alternating opened and closed white spruce forests blending to opened and closed black spruce forests. Without birch the boreal forest would resemble a menage of chimneys, stove pipes, and black zip-ties, but it becomes dominated by yellow in the fall because of birch. Under the trees in the autumn, lichens proliferate between the spruce trees and shrubs mixed with mosses—all amber, russet, and yellow. Lowbush cranberries' leaves burn-yellow, and tamarack, once blue-green in color, dazzle golden.

I swatted a bumble bee. The day looked yellow—the happy side of yellow. The sun looked yellow too; it always does to me, but it's not. Scientist say the direct light of the sun is green. Green? But it appears yellow.

Yellow is happy and present most everywhere in the natural world and is one of the colors favored by artists. Alaska artist Fred Machetanz many times used yellow in his paintings. Paintings such as *High in the Wrangells*, *Quarry in the Fog*, and *World of the Winter Sun* all employ yellow in different and fascinating ways. Others of his use yellow as well, often interpreting the sunlight's affect as yellow. His most dramatic use of yellow may be in *Alaskan Gold*. The scene is looking across Wasilla Lake to Pioneer Peak and the Chugach Mountains and a golden birch forest, the lake water reflecting the trees. The foreground and focus of the painting, in life-size rendering, are six birch leaves in autumn yellow. Machetanz wrote in his book *The Alaskan*

Paintings of Fred Machetanz: "As important as the color in this painting is the pattern and design." Step beneath a birch tree in September and look outward through the leaves and you are there in Machetanz's painting.

Yellow is a coveted color. In the late 1800s, dairy farmers were threatened by the new product oleomargarine and spent decades battling against its production and distribution. Natural butter is a pale yellow, so margarine producers colored their product yellow, and the farmers fought back. In Minnesota it was illegal to sell yellow margarine into the 1960s.

Why do I mention all this about yellow? Well, it appears some of us see more yellow as we age. Thank goodness for yellow. I like it.

This sounds obvious, but a tree is alive and eats and drinks like everything else living. Leaves reach beyond branches seeking energy, breathing through tiny holes, taking in carbon dioxide, and exhaling oxygen. When autumn arrives, the water flowing through the branch from the roots is blocked to the leaves, so the leaf begins to die.

Maybe trees talk to one another too. Robin Wall Kimmerer in *Braiding Sweetgrass* writes: "There is now compelling evidence that our elders were right—the trees are talking to one another. They communicate via pheromones, hormone-like compounds that are wafted on the breeze, laden with meaning." Likely so. I can imagine the panic when I show up with a chainsaw or whenever a birch sees a beaver shuffle up the river bank.

There is a creek upriver where I like to fish for grayling. I will occasionally clear out a fallen log so I can get a little farther upstream. I'll putt up to a log crossing the stream and pull the log downstream to open a passageway for my boat or accomplish the same by cutting a swath. During breakup and the flooding in the spring, trees are swept way. It's so odd, though, that trees keep falling across the stream. If I remove a tree, another takes its place. Maybe they send a message to one another: "When it's time to go, drop one into the stream. Keep him away."

Birch is my favorite tree. Besides its beauty, it can be a fire break of sorts during a forest fire. It's home to birds and insects, it makes excellent firewood, its bark is food for moose, and it is treasured playground equipment in the wilderness. Robert Frost had this to say in "Birches":

> Clear to the ground. He always kept his poise
> To the top branches, climbing carefully
> With the same pains you use to fill a cup
> Up to the brim, and even above the brim.
> Then he flung outward, feet first, with a swish,
> Kicking his way down through the air to the ground.
> So was I once myself a swinger of birches.

All of our sons were swingers of birches, as was Doylanne and I. Birch once dominated our clearing in the boreal forest. The boys climbed them all, even the ones too small to be safely scaled. A favorite photo from the early years at the cabin when the boys were young is of Jake, the youngest, posing on the deck of the cabin. If you pull back and take in the full scene, far up a birch is Jack standing much too high in the tree on a birch limb. Whenever I see that photo, I still yell at Jack.

22

SOLITUDE

I WALKED BACK THROUGH the yard and counted the trees either lost to me or to beavers. I counted seventy trees. Many of them became house logs, the rest firewood. I killed the spruce; beavers killed the birch. I grabbed an armload of brush from the edge of the clearing and dragged it to the old cabin site where I was dumping the debris to rot and make new soil.

Near an old rotting and abandoned log outhouse, one I built in the late 1980s, near the edge of the clearing, stood the biggest birch on the property, its trunk at least two feet in diameter. I didn't see evidence a beaver had chewed on it. Not yet. I had silly thoughts about this tree and the others in the yard. Was it lonely? Did birch give themselves to beavers? Is it all consensual? Do trees weep for one another? Die alone? Does it consider the beaver, man, or owl to be the boreal forest's greatest predator? Seems nonsensical but I wondered.

This large birch enjoyed a view of the entire homestead. What messages was it sending and receiving? I know I don't have the capacity to learn what goes on in the natural world, certainly not. Aldo Leopold put it this way: "Only the mountain has lived long enough to listen objectively to the howl of the wolf." Perhaps I could work a bit harder to understand more of nature.

I could work harder at learning about people, too, asking similar questions about them, certainly working harder to maintain connections with family and friends.

The fortunate among us have nurturing friends and family until the end. Researchers say the broader our social network, the happier and healthier we will be as we age. This network includes family, of course. Sadly, though, family can drift away over time. We die, move away, get mad, or become incapacitated by illness. Family members cause a lot of stress too. There are lots of causes for conflict: communications, habits, lifestyle choices, values, politics, religion—to name some. Friends move on as well. The number of close friends we have decreases over time. It's not solely the fault of our family and friends that we end up alone. We drive people away or pull away. Regardless of the reason, old people are often alone.

The woodstove popped, and I heard Doylanne fall off to sleep. The moon was in the window at the back of the cabin. A birch branch waved through the glass. It's at night when I know how small we are. The cabin would fit in our front yard at home in town, and here it sits in the Alaska wilderness, a small stack of sticks in the world's boreal forest, a bubble in the world's oceans. I experience smallness and isolation here. We are on our own with our bottles of pills lining a small shelf and filling a plastic tub stored beneath the bed.

We need those pills.

People over age sixty-five consume nearly one-third of all medications in the United States. I swallow my share. Medications are the single most important health care technology in preventing illness, disability, and death for old folks. Drugs keep us alive, and also make it possible for us to venture hundreds of miles away from town. My pill organizer sat on the window sill illuminated by the moon.

Doylanne sat up in bed. "I hear a noise." Something moved. I heard a crackle. Big or little? A rodent or a bear. I couldn't tell. She slid out of bed and grabbed a flashlight and went to the back-wall window. "It's a bear," she said.

I jumped out of bed and joined her. A large black bear walked beneath us and bounded onto the cabin deck. It stopped at a window and looked in. To me the window is a barrier, a sufficient barrier; to Doylanne it's nothing. The bear walked to the front of the cabin, still on the deck. I dropped to the woodstove and added wood. "Do you think it's eaten anything?" Doylanne asked, our litmus test for trouble. If a bear found food, it might become a problem.

"What's out there to eat?" I asked. I couldn't think of anything. At the back corner was a tool bench and at the front corner was a locked freezer. The freezer did have food inside, but it was clean and locked. "Let's see what it does." Ten minutes later it ambled off into the darkness. Doylanne trembled. She took photos, shaky ones, even from inside a log cabin. She worked hard to keep bears away.

We lived in the cabin like we would in a tent camp. We kept the food cooler inside the cabin; we cleaned the freezer daily; we washed all food and beverage cans before crushing them and placing them in a closed garbage can. We burned all food remains. We hauled out all garbage at the end of each trip. We lived this way because Doylanne's acutely afraid of bears, and I don't like killing them.

"Let's get back to bed. Let's try. I want to get a couple trees in the morning." We both lay awake listening for the bear. My loaded rifle rested on a gun rack above the bed.

Finally, we drifted off and slept in.

In a small dish on the table were seven pills when I sat for breakfast, my morning medication. Doylanne put them there for me. I gulped all the pills together and followed with coffee.

"Will you walk me to the outhouse this morning?" I did, carrying a can of bear spray and a handgun. Squirrels greeted us along the trail.

After our morning chores, I pulled away from the bank and putted to the other side of the river upstream from the cabin where dead trees stood upright. Doylanne watched me and called before I could fire up the chainsaw. The walkie-talkie squeaked.

"Hello there."

"Eric, I hear noises behind me."

It didn't seem likely a bear would be there. Late morning, bright day, lots of noise. "Okay, go back to the cabin, and I'll be there soon."

I went right back, and on the way up the short trail from the boat to the cabin yard, I picked up a shredded magazine left in a lawn chair. I carried a gun the rest of the day and stood by as armed guard when Doylanne harvested more potatoes.

I chopped firewood in the afternoon and thought about when our four sons ran through the yard years before. We had rules like don't go beyond the clearing, don't climb too high in a tree, don't hit one another, stay away from the river bank. The little boys, ages four and six, wore bells on their shoes so we could hear them. The older boys, ten and twelve, were expected to be in charge and on guard. Once Jack, our oldest, came back to the cabin after a run to the outhouse, "I saw a black bear on the trail," he said. We all turned to him. "I shooed it away." We set stricter rules. Let us know before going to the outhouse.

"Mountain's coming out," Doylanne said, a cue to come to the cabin and sit on the deck and watch the river and the mountain. She waited for me. I once was asked, "What do you do up there?" If I did nothing but sit on the deck and watch Denali morph before my eyes I would have done enough. Jonathan Waterman wrote in *In the Shadow of Denali:* "I was lost in Denali fantasy. I should have been through with the mountain, but it had captured me more thoroughly than a lover." We constantly look to the mesmerizing mountain and evaluate its clarity. On this day, it dazzled.

We ate dinner on the deck in our jackets and knit hats and were joined by eagles, beavers, ducks, and squirrels. Near dark two owls began to hoot. We didn't hear from bears, wolves, or moose, but they were probably present, being quiet during the dinner hour.

"Know something different here, Doylanne. I don't nap."

"I noticed. Take your meds tonight?" Doylanne asked.

I wasn't taking anything for what was hurting me at the moment, my lower back and the stinging pains shooting through my right leg. My medications were all about a heart attack.

In the morning I started work on the outhouse. This

was to be Doylanne's place. We'd have a his and hers, one upriver and one downriver. I brought in a metal door with a large glass window from our house in town. The structure would be all white spruce milled from dead trees near the cabin. I'd done the milling work in May, so my work would be getting the boards to the right size and building.

I cleared an area for the outhouse and roughly marked out where the foundation would go. I faced a challenge. A goal was not to cut down any trees, but there was a three-inch-in-diameter spruce growing at the edge of the foundation. "We'll see little tree," I said. I was determined to let it live if it didn't pose too big a problem. I dug the hole, about three-by-three and five feet deep. Once I broke through the active layer of roots, the digging was easy. The soil held loosely together with sewing thread roots—some strands like spider silk—surrounding, intertwining, and merging.

I winched in logs for the foundation.

The toilet seat would end up about four feet above ground level. I framed the building with two-by-fours and two-by-twos and used metal for the roof. I sided it with one-inch boards ranging from eight to fourteen inches in width using a lap-siding style. I installed the toilet seat (one I'd painted and given to Doylanne as a Christmas present) and installed the door and . . . done! It took me three days to finish the project. The little tree angles out one side of the foundation and has a fighting chance.

"What's next?" Doylanne asked. We again were on the deck celebrating our new homestead addition, studying the finicky autumn sky. Weather watching is hypnotic. When the wind is resting, I can sit and watch and listen for hours. Branches pulled under by the current snap back splashing; the current gurgles, bubbles, and trickles musically before us. A duck will slide in for a landing, making a splash and a thud, usually invoking laughter. They're always landing on an aircraft carrier.

"I guess I should start looking for a moose."

"How's your back today?"

"My leg hurts the most."

"Good enough for a moose, Eric?" Another good question. I'd want the moose to be pretty close to the boat.

"I'll stay on the river," I said.

"Tell me something different."

"Do we have any pain pills?"

"Yes, but let's save them for a big one."

"Big moose?"

"No, big mistake."

"Yeah, it could happen. It's a spooky place." Back behind us to the north, I heard the drone of a large airplane, the only other human we'd heard since we left town. "Town's spooky too."

Sounds terrible, I suppose, to want to take a break from people, get out of town. I like people well enough and love many of them, and I worked my entire career in people-rich professions, but I still want to regularly get away from them.

No television, no radio, no internet makes for an amazing day. In town I'm glued to my cell phone. If I leave it at home, I am unprepared to go to town. I've turned around to get it several times. It's interesting, though, as soon as I run out of cell reception on the river, I don't care. After a day I don't even think about the phone or Facebook or Google. It's easy to leave town behind in the wilderness.

I don't like automobiles and drivers either. Cars with loony drivers make me crazy. Fifty years of driving and I've become overly sensitive to the idiocy on the road. Maybe it's an allergy. A few days before we left for the cabin, I drove a side street outside of Wasilla, a route I usually take to avoid traffic. There was a car behind me when I came to the only stop sign on the street. I stopped at the T, put on my blinker, and looked both ways. As I turned toward town, the driver behind me honked his horn, startling me. We were the only ones on the road. What in the world is the hurry? It's shameful, but what I had in mind was slamming on my brakes, pulling this pencil neck twerp out of his car, and stepping on his head. But I drove on, angry for hours. I believe it would be an advancement for mankind to remove horns from automobiles.

The guy honking his horn acted nuts. One should have

a compelling reason to honk in the state with the highest gun ownership rate in the United States. One of us was likely experiencing a mental disorder. I'll say it's him. Who would honk on a country road? But it might be me, you know what I was thinking.

Most people who experience mental health issues delay seeking help for more than a decade. Lots of people, including older people, deal with it. As bad as all this is, it gets worse because mental illness affects those around the afflicted. Work, relationships, and physical health are all impacted, and it goes on and on with linkages among mental health, behavioral health, substance abuse, disease, suicide, health care, medications, and health care costs.

I've never heard a horn in the wilderness. Well, I suppose not true. Two honkers had recently flown over and I didn't mind.

"How are you going to hunt today?"

"Drift downriver. What will you do?"

"Get some potatoes." We have a small raised garden near the cabin of river soil, leaves, food scraps, coffee grounds, egg shells, and firewood ash. Potato is our only vegetable. We plant near the end of May and the garden is left unattended until we harvest in September. Weeds take over and the garden becomes unrecognizable. This country isn't the best for gardening. People in the north with good gardens work hard at it. We couldn't, so we weren't optimistic the first year we tried, but the yield was okay, so we did it again. We harvest enough golf ball- to baseball-sized potatoes to get us through our trip and still take a few to town.

I pushed away from the bank and poured coffee from a thermos. I placed my rifle in the bow so I could easily reach it. A beaver swam the river ahead of me. I planned to drift for a few hours, stay off the bank with the push pole, and occasionally use a bull call to see if one would standup or step out in the open, a proven strategy, and if I stayed in the boat, I wouldn't wander off too far in the woods. I searched into the trees with binoculars. Several of the local creatures showed up but not the one I looked for.

A beaver paddled in front of me and climbed onto a beach with thick willow growth. I drifted by and encountered another beaver. I watched it pull a willow branch under a sweeper. What's it with beavers? It came out from under the sweeper and dove, smacking its tail, making a sound like a book dropping to a library floor.

It came to me, a diagnosis. They're hoarders. Beavers are hoarders. Obviously, they're obsessive-compulsive. Leonard Lee Rue III in *The World of the Beaver* wrote "Dam building is actually a compulsion with beavers." No doubt. So maybe it wasn't their fault. They can't help themselves.

I've been around beavers for more than thirty years, climbing and traversing their dams. Because of them, many believe, wetland habitats exist. Beavers create places for swans to land and raise their cygnets. Beavers do good things.

In *Eager: The Surprising, Secret Life of Beavers and Why They Matter*, Ben Goldfarb describes why beavers are important to the natural world: "Aquatic insects shelter in the nooks and crannies of dams and lodges. Ducks nest in the grasses that spring up around pond fringes. Songbirds perch in coppicing willows. Biologists have discovered that turtles and lizards are more abundant near beaver ponds." Beavers build community housing, develop close social bonds, take care of their kits, and are loyal to their own. I didn't dislike beavers, but I was considering killing a bunch of them, but I hadn't shot any yet.

No moose walked out to see me. I cruised back to the cabin

We again sat on the deck amid gold coins, pearls, and diamond-leaden trinkets, the river sparkling and the sun about to drop below the trees. Two swans appeared overhead and landed downriver. I heard them slide to a stop. They immediately began honking.

"Isn't it interesting that one inch of candle melts in an hour," I said.

"Yes, it is. A candle melts at the rate sand runs in an hourglass. We think about different things here at the cabin, don't we. I guess that's what solitude does," she said.

23

Cranberries

I KICKED BACK ON THE deck and watched Denali emerge and fill the frame and resolved this was the end of my day. I wasn't moving. I'd wait for the evening wildlife action to begin.

Doylanne saw it first. The dot in the pale sky became a bald eagle. We knew this nosy eagle, and it knew us. It floated over and circled twice and sailed beyond the trees. Minutes later I saw it hundreds of yards away, gliding back upstream. Two swans appeared on an upriver beach a quarter mile away. A pair of teals weaved among the sweepers. Gray jays, squirrels, and mice appeared. Near dark, owls began to hoot, and I began to worry about the squirrels.

"You okay, Doylanne?" I asked. She had her physical ailments too.

"My knee's sore today."

She often stopped and grimaced after climbing the deck stairs. I watched Denali change faces, and I wondered about why, as in: why are we here when we hurt so much? My back hurt from years of lifting; my neck hurt from falls and contortions; my nose was constricted from elbows thrown my way; my limbs ached from once broken appendages. By our mid-sixties our skin is wrinkling, our joints wearing, our metabolism slowing, our heart failing, our senses waning, and we need to go to the bathroom a lot. The news is not so good.

We heard a crash upstream. We looked up toward the old outhouse hidden in the trees. Shortly after, a birch, probably eight inches in diameter floated before us. A beaver claimed another victim.

"You should get the tree for firewood," Doylanne said. Thirty minutes later I was back at the deck with a birch tied off to the boat, wondering if it would be there in the morning or would it disappear like Hemingway's fish.

I've noticed the wilderness brings out the philosophical and esoteric questions, not the answers, just the questions. For instance, does anybody really know where they are? Do we know the true nature of where we live? Sure, we have an address. As for me, I'm writing this at home about ten miles from Wasilla, and this location has been bestowed an address. I can find it on a map, on Google Earth, and instantly on my iPhone. So I know my location but not where I am. I suspect few of us know because we don't look. We spend years only focused on the hood ornament. We won't take the time to look and learn.

The next morning we drifted to the mouth of our river where we anchored and sat in the sun to let time pass before heading back upstream. After coffee, we left, and a few turns up, cruising on step about fifteen miles an hour, we jumped two small bulls standing on a beach.

"Take it," I said to Doylanne as I pushed through the boat door to the bow. Doylanne jumped in my seat. The moose ran toward the trees. I tried to get a moose in my scope. Doylanne killed the engine. I could have shot a moose likely, but probably a gut shot or a wound shot, ruining the day for all of us. I couldn't get an acceptable shot so I didn't take one.

"Pull over here to the bank, Doylanne." I tied off to a willow. "We'll wait here a while." We sat in the boat for nearly an hour hoping a moose would walk out onto the beach. "Let's go up here and look for berries. We can watch from up there." We were against a high bank with large white spruce trees and lots of cranberries. We picked and watched and talked of being in two worlds. Now and then. A few decades before I would have attempted a shot and done it well. In seconds the rifle would have been fired and the moose lay dead or dying while we beached the boat and walked to it and finished it. If I missed or passed on the shot, we would have hung in the river watching but only for minutes before jumping back on step looking for another. Cranberries wouldn't be in the equation. Now when I hunt, I make myself available to get a moose. I don't so much look any more, only get out there so maybe one will offer himself up for the freezer. I still get moose but not nearly as many. Those are the two worlds. I'd now rather watch and admire than take.

"Let's go home." Doylanne nodded. She was happy with berries.

I can't do what I once could, none of us can. This reality is amplified because the trip to our homestead and the experiences once there are so unforgiving. What's required to get up the rivers and what's needed to safely experience the wilderness hasn't changed, only we've changed. If I hunt, I must carry a moose. If I pick berries, I must climb a bank. If I want coffee, I must start a fire. If I want a warm cabin, I must gather firewood. It's become quite a physical challenge. Between Doylanne and I, we suffer from arthritis, like lots of people; heart disease, which is the leading killer of those over sixty-five; cancer, the second leading killer; osteoporosis, a condition faced by more than fifty million Americans over fifty; diabetes, affecting more than 25 percent of those over sixty-five; an autoimmune disorder, a condition making days miserable; and many of the other bad actors like periodic episodes of influenza, pneumonia, aching teeth and gums, and aches and pains from falls and sprains. In other words, we're like most people sixty-five and older: we live with conditions. It's best not to think of back then, when we could do everything. If we spend much time there, we'll do nothing.

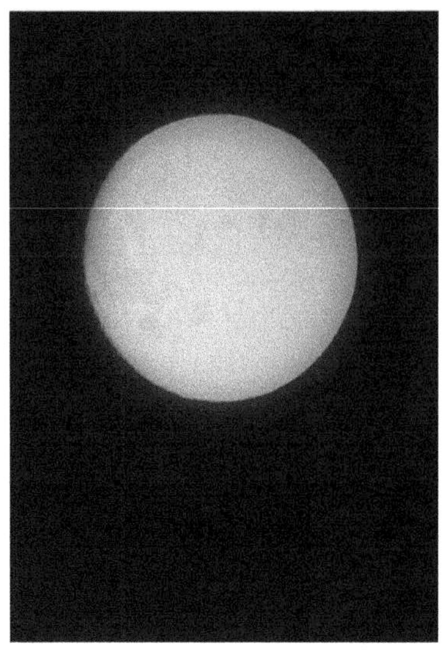

24

Night Time

We hiked to King Beaver Pond and sat together on a ledge looking out over the water, the lodge directly in front of us and the taiga stretching beyond. I carried a rifle, a handgun, and bear spray. A reddish-brown beaver, the rodent with the special tail, cruised near the end of the pond but there was no action near the lodge. Beavers grow old, up to twenty-four years in the wild. A long time for a sixty-pound vegetarian without fangs. It probably knew we were there. Beavers are beautiful animals lacking the respect they deserve. They're sort of the second team of animals in the north, I suppose, but their value to the nineteenth-century North American economy and to the environment is undeniable. They've also kept people alive, providing the second or third choice for meat. From *On the Edge of Nowhere*, a memoir of James Huntington told to Lawrence Elliott: "Take beaver. They're nice and fat in the winter and make a wonderful meal. But if you get one, you've really earned that meal. Beavers build elaborate rooms and tunnels under the ice, and it takes a pen set, a kind of trap, and a lot of hard work to trap them. But when you're hungry and go hacking through the ice looking for food, chances are they'll slip away down an escape tunnel while you're freezing on the bank and wondering where they are. If you shoot one it had better be a big one; the others will stay down until the ice is out of the river."

The beaver at the end of the pond swam toward us,

veered to the lodge, slapped its flat tail, and disappeared. We waited, hoping the beaver would surface but didn't see it again.

"The beaver remembers us, maybe," I said. Doylanne watched the hut but didn't immediately respond. I picked at cranberries and looked through the black spruce for a moose.

"Why wouldn't it?" She answered. Yes, why wouldn't it? It's still alive because of its awareness.

We hiked back to the cabin, the path covered in leaves, and finished the evening on the cabin deck. We waited for the moon to break above the trees and shine on the river.

"Would you put the ladder beneath the window?" Doylanne liked having a five-foot folding aluminum ladder below the west window at the back of the cabin. She thought the ladder deterred any bear considering the window as an entrance. Seemed ironic, though, using a ladder.

"Think I'll take a shower," I said.

Inside the cabin, I started a gasoline two-mantle lantern and added wood to the stove while Doylanne started on dinner and warmed a pan of water for my shower.

Behind the cabin stood the woodshed and shower frame. I'd built the framework and used a brown polyurethane tarp to encircle the shower space to provide privacy. A three-gallon container with a shower head served as the water source. I mixed hot and cold river water.

"Be right back," I said. I stripped in the cold with a slight breeze from the south. I opened the shower nozzle and went for it. Three minutes later I finished. I wrapped myself in a towel and waddled to the cabin.

Doylanne showered an hour later and dashed to the cabin. I don't dash anymore. Truthfully, I am older than she is, but three months shouldn't make so much difference.

I've noticed I wait more than I did before, much more cautious. I wait for Doylanne to get up first, start the coffee, make breakfast, read her daily list. I wait to check the weather before committing to a fishing trip or a building project. I wait for the opinion of others before embarking on a new adventure. Might be wisdom at work—possibly—or insecurity.

I sat on the edge of the bed. I poked at my belly, a soft round armload a granddaughter calls a marshmallow and what Friedrich Nietzsche said was the reason man does not "readily take himself to be a god."

I described the shed again. "It'll be a beauty. Pretty standard with a gable roof with room for a loft. It'll take lots of boards to frame it. I think I'll lap side the front and board and batten the other walls. A four-foot door and a couple windows."

I laid back in bed and grabbed a book. The lantern light was not quite enough for reading so I used a flashlight.

"A shed might be a two-year project," I said.

We ate popcorn and read until after midnight. The wind picked up and we heard leaves in the air. "Doylanne, I think I'll step out for a while."

"Go outside?"

"To the edge of the yard to watch and listen." I stepped out onto the deck, and the moon was visible through light clouds. Solar lights lit up the deck and a pathway to the boat. I walked off into the woods to pee and from the dark looked back at the cabin. A pane of light from the front wall window angled downward and stopped in darkness, a single shard in a remote forest.

The moon was a letter C dangling at ten o'clock, the black river casting the shape of a snake. I walked to the giant birch at the back of the yard and sat and listened to a growing breeze. The chill of September squashed the mosquitoes, so it seemed I sat alone, but I knew better. Squirrels hid quietly in the trees, rodents curled in grass tunnels, and birds sat silent, their beaks under their wings so not to peep. Night seems more noisy than day. The nocturnal predators were stirring, carrying their own sounds. Darkness amplifies sound. Was an owl pouncing on a mouse or a bear pawing a rotten tree and slurping ants? The lantern blazed in the cabin. I could see in from where I sat. A bar of yellow light pierced the darkness for several feet beyond the cabin's four windows until it vanished into the ground. Through the shards of light, an occasional amber leaf floated and I imagined sometimes a confused mosquito got caught in the glare. The most common invader was the moth. Butterflies hid.

My brother and I built the structure while on a wild adventure in the late 1980s. Doylanne and I, with the help of our sons and friends, finished the cabin a little bit at a time. All the logs were taken within a few hundred feet and winched to the building site with a chainsaw winch. Every log was lifted into place by the strength of neophytes fulfilling a dream.

Standing in the dark looking backward is what we all often do in life. I'm not alone in this I know. A review of only the good is temporarily enjoyable but probably not too helpful. If we review only the bad, we feel sad and maybe even cringe, not helpful either. I haven't found a way to filter out the extremes. I have noticed, though, when at the cabin, I don't spend nearly as much time playing movie reels in my head. I'm much too busy thinking about "what's next" and "what's out there."

A thin white moonbeam ran diagonally across the river. I'd been up in the middle of the night enough times to know the moon would shine on the upriver stretch eventually. The cabin was in the middle of a long half circle of river. In the early evening the moon shone on the downriver half, in the wee morning the other half. My binoculars were standard issue—ten by forty-two, meaning an object appeared ten times larger than it would with the naked eye and the lens allowed decent light at night. Through the darkness, I magnified the sliver of moon 239,000 miles away. I looked but couldn't see anyone sitting there.

I finally grew too cold and went inside and wedged against pillows with *Of Wolves and Men* and read until the lantern began to sputter.

I awakened to Doylanne squeezing my arm. Little steps, a mouse, perhaps, on the deck near the front door woke her. Not worthy of getting up to look. It couldn't do any harm.

It began gnawing. What was it chewing on? When I woke, it still gnawed, but it was dark, and I couldn't get a proper angle out the front window for a view. I opened the front door, and there was a nearly severed handle of our broom.

The wilderness is alive at night. Obviously, it's easier to avoid getting eaten when you can't be seen, so animals—little and big ones—search for food in the dark. So, although the little creatures are obscured in the dark, their predators can also hide and ambush dinner more easily. The little mouse on my deck was looking for food and ate my broom. I suppose it had a reason. I hoped it successfully retreated to its home under the cabin.

Animals only kill for a reason related to survival. French post-impressionist painter Henri Rousseau, who said he had "no teacher but nature," never left France, but he knew something about wild animals: the fact they are wild doesn't make them indiscriminate killers. Among his paintings are wilderness depictions, the most famous perhaps being *The Sleeping Gypsy*. I've only seen online versions of the painting (Museum of Modern Art, New York City), but I was struck by its wilderness insight: animals eat when they're hungry and only when the meal's on their menu. His portrayal of a lion standing near a sleeping woman on a moonlit night strikes a truthful chord. A woman gypsy is sleeping on sand, a large waterway is in the background with mountains beyond the water. The night sky is clear with stars waking, and a full moon dangles at two o'clock. The marking on the moon resembles a man's face. Standing near and beyond the women is a lion sniffing the sand. The woman, herself wild, sleeping in the open, is not prey. The lion has stopped by to visit, not to harm.

The cabin, built on a popular animal pathway, has frequent visitors, most of them during the night when we're sleeping. We interact with only a few. If we slept on the deck in the open under the moon with the drifting amber leaves, we would still not hear them all. They would come and go, and if not too hungry, would leave us alone.

25

Fire

The cabin's front door is made of boards two inches thick. Inside, to the left, is a copper countertop for whatever needs to be immediately unloaded after entering. Four inches away to the left is the apartment-sized propane cooking range. Still to the left is the airtight, cast iron woodstove. Looking to the right from the doorway are shelves with dishes, cups, glasses, and utensils and the kitchen sink. Beyond the sink is the bed. On the back wall is a bookshelf and hanging near is a collection of toys: BB guns, a wooden chainsaw, and a spear. Little boy high-top tennis shoes dangle from a nail. Thirty years passes in a glance.

Doylanne knelt before the woodstove, arranging wood. I used to get up first to stoke or start the fire and get coffee going. Now, Doylanne sometimes gets impatient and beats me to it. I hear her turn in bed, exhale, exhale again. If I stay put, lying still, she'll relent and get up first. After I hear the coffee water nearing the whistle, I'll say, "Oh, I didn't know you were up." She always smiles at playful subterfuge. Coffee time is time to plan the day, same as it is in town.

"What do you want for breakfast?" Doylanne asked.

"How long does it take to make oatmeal?"

"Same as yesterday. You getting over your soreness?"

"Not gone, but I'm okay. I want to hike to the ridge behind the cabin. Be back well before dinner time. I'll take a walkie-talkie." The scratches on my face still hadn't healed. "Want to go?"

She stayed at the cabin. I walked to the end of King Beaver pond and turned right on the same track I took when

I became lost in the dark. Autumn had completely taken over the forest. I wove through the trees and up a ridge to an overlook facing south toward the mountains. The cabin was hidden, but I could easily see the line of spruce waving near the river. Here I also met the remains of the destruction, charred trees crisscrossing one another, creating a swath more than one hundred yards wide. The remains of forest fires—dead logs scattered like dropped match sticks—influence animal movement across the land. The fire was ten years old, and new growth rose above the first layer of logs. Fresh food.

Trees and flowers grow old, too—furrowed and rough, disappointing both moose and moose hunters. Moose don't like to eat old plants. Maybe it's the toughness of the older willow bark or the tartness of the leaves from the older trees, but moose move on in search of newness when the forest goes old. A fire can restore the freshness. Hunters know moose are attracted to the new growth after a fire, so some track fires. After nature's forest purge, small plants grow back quickly. Plants survive the fire, particularly the smallest plants, and seeds survive, so growth is rapid and both moose and hunters return to a fire site within a few years. For trees in our area, though, the growth after a fire is unfairly slow. Forests need to recycle in one manner or another. In most places now, because of all the people and structures, forest management involving logging, selective logging and culling might be the best approach. In other places, allowing the fire to run its course and burn out makes the most sense. In July 2019 the largest fire in the United States raged near Livingood, Alaska, north of Fairbanks. The Hess Creek Fire by mid-July had consumed more than 172,000 acres, about 269 square miles. Now in mid-August, as this story's being written, it's still burning in the wilderness and will burn until nature stops it. When we can, allowing nature to handle wildfires is the best course.

Purging is a natural phenomenon most of us frequently attempt in one way or another. It can make things right. When I worked as a school principal, I cleaned my desk most afternoons, swept its top into two desk drawers, one drawer for those potential heartbreaks or lawsuits needing to be addressed the next day, the other for "maybe I'll do it" or "maybe it'll eventually get lost forever in the pile." I tried to enter the building every day with a new game face and new beginning. It was a goal.

One September, not too many years before, our third son and I picked our way through thick forest, heading toward light several hundred feet ahead. Our pants gathered thorns from thigh-high roses, stickers piercing my legs through my jeans. We were checking out property, and I was growing excited, liking everything so far. The trees were a mix of paper birch and white spruce with patches of willow. We stepped on and over lichens, fungi, moss, and wove through chest-high cranberry plants. We were a few miles from the cabin.

"Look here, Dad."

At his feet was a large pile of bear scat. I poked around in the pile, wondering if I'd recognize anything. Didn't see anything I knew about. We pushed our way through the willow to the edge of a shining lake. We climbed on logs to improve the view. Before us was a lake covered with waterfowl. I stopped counting swans at twenty. To our left and to the south was Denali, but it wasn't visible from where I stood. Straight ahead and to the right were rolling hills. Yeah, I was happy with this prospect.

"This'll do, do you think?"

"Beautiful, Dad."

Jed and I staked the land.

The following May, I showed Doylanne the corner posts on the new property. We hiked the property line twice. The birch and willow leaves weren't fully developed, curled like infant hands. The early blue bells bloomed and the blossoms of the highbush cranberry with fingernail-sized pearl petals brightened the underbrush.

"I think this would be a nice cabin spot," I said.

"Yes, and maybe the outhouse here," she said. She walked over to a slight incline with a spectacular view of the lake. "And a shed maybe between here and the river."

A few weeks later, back in town, I saw the news story

in the *Fairbanks News Miner.* Wildfires were scorching the interior and one raged near our cabin and new property. I clicked to the Alaska Interagency Coordination Center website, and there it was: a fire seethed where Doylanne and I had stood weeks before. The map pinpointed the location. I studied the map, expanded the map. I knew many of the contours personally.

"Oh no." Doylanne said.

"Maybe the map is off a bit," I said, but didn't believe it. I called the AICC and they confirmed an active fire at the coordinates I gave them. There were, they told me, firefighters in the area protecting the few cabins near there. So we watched for nearly two weeks until the fire status was downgraded, and we quit checking but kept worrying.

When Doylanne and I headed to the woods in September, we didn't know what damage we might find. We thought the cabin probably survived. We hoped. The cabin was there, and a fire crew saved it. They'd cut a swath around the cabin, but like fires go, a large white spruce burned in front of the cabin, I guess ignited by flying ashes. Except for a couple acres near the river, the property Jed and I staked burned to the ground.

It will not grow back in our lifetimes. I still, at times, in a reoccurring dream, see the land as it was, the tall thick birch and straight spruce. The dreams end the same: trees fading in a maze.

The Camp Fire in California in 2018 was the deadliest fire in the last one hundred years in America. I was shocked they couldn't contain it. Aren't we capable of accomplishing anything we want? Ours was tiny in comparison to the Camp Fire, and the comparative loss minuscule, but it still hurt.

Our fire blazed nearly ten years ago. All summers since have been hotter and dryer, the sky darkened with smoke from hundreds of miles away. Isn't it fascinating and strange we can smell a tree burned so many miles away? A whiff of wildfire smoke can stir odd emotions and sometimes apocalyptic visions. We can't stop what blows our way.

26

IMAGINING THE WORST

I CALLED DOYLANNE ON THE walkie-talkie. She still worked on the morning dishes.

"I'm going to the sausage trees."

"Be careful."

If I got through the burn and hiked another mile, I would come to a meadow the size of a small city. Looking back to the south was a spectacular view of Denali and the Alaska range. I headed that way. I stepped into the burn debris and began climbing over and through the fallen trees twisted and charred like guard rails after a nasty crash. When I brushed against them, they left black scars on my clothing. I soon sat exhausted on a mostly burned log, thinking about moose.

What does a moose do in a forest fire? I imagine them sprinting away, fleeing the country, but based on studies of collared moose, scientists say they flee from flames but don't leave the area of the fire. Many moose die, but survivors hang in the fringes after the blaze, feeding on what plant life remains. Unburned vegetation provides enough food and cover for the moose to stay in the area. So moose only run as far as they must and stop and live near the edges. Scientists have found moose often aren't where the fires are anyway. Fires tend to explode in old forests, so moose aren't there when the fire begins. The moose move on because the food is old.

It was obvious moose weren't walking around in this jungle-gym of trees. They'd break a leg in a hurry, and even with healthy legs, they wouldn't be able to run from a wolf. I was about to break one of mine if I wasn't careful. Step over this log, crawl under another, twist around another. I faced a Gordian knot. I needed a chainsaw.

I kept on through the broken and tangled trees to a stand of thin birch. After a short hike through the birch, the forest changed to black spruce and muskeg. I knew what was out there so kept on northward, taking long careful strides over the spongy muskeg. I stopped after every few steps to rest and went on until I arrived at the meadow engulfing a large blue sparkling pond, water breaking with the breeze, covered with dozens of trumpeter swans.

About noon, I called Doylanne again.

"I'll be back well before dark. It'll take me two hours to get back. No, I won't shoot anything. Hey, light a candle. I'll call in an hour."

With binoculars, I scanned the subarctic grassland encircling the pond. Before me were hundreds of acres of bluejoint reed grass two to four feet tall. The red tops blending with russet tops waving in the breeze looked like a home for plains bison, or its spikelets resembled wheat fields in the Midwest. I'd seen this grass in southcentral Alaska, too, but never an expanse like this. I imagined the American west I'd read about as a child. I settled against a black spruce. The sky's pale complexion blended white at the tops of the spruce at the horizon. A hawk circled near the center of the meadow.

When in town, I dream of these moments. They motivate me over the long winter to return to the cabin and hike deep into the woods. I closed my eyes and listened to thc wind and the constant rustling. A woodpecker behind me joined in the music.

I called Doylanne but no answer.

At the far side of the meadow, to the east, was a survey monument the size of a coaster marking a property line. Near the survey monument would be the faint remains of an airstrip I'd built with the help of Doylanne and our sons thirty years before, an air strip used only a couple times by my brother, Charles, in his Piper Cub. I'd watched this grassland before.

I called Doylanne again. She didn't answer.

I gathered my gear and walked east to see if I could find any sign of the township line, an imaginary line marking the relative north and south locations of townships in a U.S. public land survey. The name's a bit misleading because no one could have ever envisioned a town here. The line was indeed imaginary, never cleared, but I'd traveled it several times through the years. I stopped when it was near and checked the GPS. I was there but I didn't see any sign. I looked for a blazed tree or small black spruce stump.

Sandhill cranes called overhead. I headed south back toward the cabin. At the wide strip of burned forest, I corrected to the west to meet the line I'd walked to get to the fire remains and stepped again into the snarled logs. Midway through I rested.

I called again. No answer. Ever notice animals in stress flare their nostrils? I began to worry.

I picked up my pace, crawling again through and over logs resembling spider legs, but I had to rest. Drops of sweat fell on the soot and streaked the logs. I wasn't finding oxygen. I stumbled out of the logs and quickly came to the ridge where I could see a long narrow horseshoe lake below rimmed with birch and spruce forest extending to near the river. I veered more to the south to hike along the ridge to descend to another meadow I would cross to get to King Beaver Pond. Before descending the ridge, I sat and called. No answer.

I could hear individual leaves land around me, on my shoulders, my head, my legs, but also on the ground around me, each its own soft final landing. I closed my eyes and said "no, no, no" to drive thoughts away, and the leaves dropped and covered my boots, my knees, my chest, and only my head remained above the amber and russet leaves. I saw a man on horseback ride up to a man buried up to his neck in the sand and ride away. I saw a man frozen in the ice. I saw a man floating in the sea, twirling like a pinwheel before disappearing.

I called again and she answered. She'd been napping.

"Did you light a candle?"

"No."

"I said I'd call in an hour."

"Sorry."

I laid back amid dwarf dogwood, catching my breath. I filled my lungs, sweat drying on my face.

Looking straight up to the light clouds, I saw v-formations of sandhill cranes, and to my left near two o'clock in the sky, a jet contrail too high to be from a Fairbanks flight, maybe going to Anchorage or Seattle, maybe the Far East. Incongruity is fascinating. I had feet planted in two worlds with knowledge of each and both so radically different from one another, in a real-world sense as well as symbolically: the jetliner, a great technological achievement, and the crane with one of the oldest fossil records of any existing bird. A fossil thought to be ten million years old found in Nebraska belongs to a crane or its prehistoric cousin. Here in the deep woods, I experienced both now and then.

We certainly connect with phenomena larger than ourselves. We read religious texts, watch the stars, imagine unknown worlds and cultures, and reconstruct our own lives. The latter is the easiest and for many the most pleasurable. Reminiscing our own past connects us with branches of the tree most of us know little about. Our family comprises its own unexplored universe.

Gerontologists say looking back can be good for seniors. For starters, the exercise preserves family history. Life's too busy for most of us to tell our children our special stories. Looking back can improve our outlook on life. Retelling happy memories makes people happy. Seniors who suffer from dementia are thought to show improvement following reminiscence therapy, a treatment using all the senses to help individuals remember events, people, and places from their past. Life reviews also help seniors with depression. The process can assist seniors work through unresolved conflicts. Experts identify lots of benefits gained from looking backward as long as there's a marked pathway returning to the present.

The sound of the sandhill cranes faded and was replaced by the sound of a growing wind from the south. I hiked the ridge to King Beaver Pond and back along the river to the cabin. Orange and yellow leaves landed on my head and shoulders. Near the river bank, upstream from the cabin, I stopped at the grave marker for our toy poodle Rocky.

We'd brought our first poodle, Princess, to the cabin years before. She didn't belong there, all of her wildness bred from her. She couldn't walk through the forest without help. She got lost in the undergrowth. Once while on a trip searching for berries, she trailed behind, the leash run through my belt loop. Doylanne hiked near me, her arms full of cranberries. The boys, loaded with cranberries, cameras, and the remnants of a picnic, followed the poodle. Occasionally, they'd reach and lift her free from the bushes. At the boat the poodle easily scampered down the bank to the boat to wait in the bow while the rest of us struggled on the incline. On the ride to the cabin, the poodle sat in the bow, near a boy, nose to the wind, ears flapping. She barked occasionally and snapped at the air, but I couldn't hear her over the outboard. She turned her head to catch her breath.

Once the boat stopped, the poodle stretched to reach the highest spot in the boat to view the water and all the activity taking place on shore. The boat had a narrow beam and low sides and two bench seats. I stopped at a small creek so the boys could make a few casts. The poodle stood with her sinewy hind legs on a bench and her front legs on the gunwale. When a fly rod moved she moved. Miraculously, the poodle never fell where pike posed her greatest danger. She looked like a black woolly worm. The mosquitoes didn't bother her much. They swarmed her at times, and she caught them by snapping in the air. She jumped at grayling. Her tail whipped like the tip of the fly rod. As the fish swam along the boat, she kept pace, jumping from the front platform to a bench seat, teetering on the gunwale. The grayling was lifted out of the water by the line, rod bowed, the barbless hook in the upper lip, dangling a few inches above the bottom of the boat within her reach. She stiffened, tail erect, nose quivering. She sniffed the glistening grayling for a few moments before it was tossed back in the stream. We occasionally missed a fish because of the poodle. Grayling bolt for the fly. If a strike coincided with the poodle crashing into the tackle box while chasing a golden dragonfly or the poodle exploding at the sight of a beaver cruising along the bank, the fish was often missed. On the final stretch to the cabin, she hid under my coat, her head poking out about chest level. Once the boat pulled up to the bank at the cabin, she dashed out of the bow, leading the way into the yard.

The white spruce grave marker for Rocky was in view of the cabin deck. Doylanne waved. I picked weeds around the marker and arranged river rocks we'd placed there. I talked to Rocky for a moment. A loud rumble caused me to look downstream. I knew what it was, a growing wind building in the trees. These gusts occurred frequently and demanded I watch. The trees bent together. At the marker, amber leaves swirled.

Somewhere else someone stood over a grave marker. Maybe at the monument I once found a hundred miles or so downriver when I was looking for a place to camp. One evening, years before, I struggled upstream with an overloaded boat and pulled in at a corner. On shore a cross lay on the ground. On the underside was a placard with a rest in peace message to a man who'd died years before. I didn't know the story about this man and still don't. I stood the marker against a tree and went back to the boat and headed upriver. I didn't want to camp there.

Doylanne swept the deck. I missed her, even after only a few hours in the woods. We'd been together nearly fifty years, forty-four of those married. When she didn't answer, I panicked among a tangle of the fallen scarred logs and blackened fire ruins.

27

Calling Home

"Let's go up the river today. It's a beautiful morning," Doylanne said.

I was for it. We left with a pack for lunch, a satellite phone, and a plan to run toward the mountains and go as far as the water allowed us.

The river picks up speed in front of our cabin and grows faster and shallower every corner upstream. In the foothills, the river bottom turns from mostly sand to mostly multicolored stones, changing the surface color. Ripples and bubbles mark the river, and the bottom is a killer on the prop and lower unit. The cinnamon beaches reach out and nearly close off the river in places. Doylanne and I go there whenever we can.

After ten minutes, we stopped at the eagle's nest up from the cabin. I idled in the river while Doylanne snapped photos. It perched on a branch near its nest. There was still only one. An eagle reaching adulthood can live more than twenty years. I putted beyond the eagle and jumped back on step. Soon we stopped at a beach we knew well, a large expanse of copper-colored sand I called Popcorn Beach. We stopped to look for pretty pieces of driftwood

Twenty-five years or so before, Jack, James, and I ran up to this spot to camp one afternoon. Doylanne and our two youngest, Jed and Jake, stayed at the cabin. The mid-July sun blazed, so once we reached the beach, the boys jumped in the river. I set up a small dome tent and sat in a lawn chair to watch the play. They rolled in the sand while

I sat in the sun until time for dinner. I planned to heat up soup left over from the night before.

Only the year before we began using CB radios. I set up a base station at the cabin and added a couple handheld radios. I called Doylanne.

"I'm setting up the stove. What you doing?"

"Making popcorn."

"Boys are in the river"

"Boys here are reading," she said.

"Popcorn sounds good." Jack dove in the river. "Hey, I'll call you right back." I walked over to the boys. "You want to go back to the cabin and have popcorn?"

We loaded the boat in minutes. We put the erect tent in the bow of the boat.

"Doylanne, make more popcorn. We're coming home." The boys toweled off and shivered and I cruised.

"Do you remember the popcorn trip?" I asked Doylanne.

"Of course."

We left Popcorn Beach and came to a significant stream emerging from the northwest. Before the mouth were the remains of an old camp. Doylanne and I walked through the camp site and found old bed springs. We left it alone and kept on upstream.

I looked for a paddle wheel I'd once seen in this river. Nearly thirty years before, I saw what was a part from a paddle boat rising above the current in the middle of the narrow river. I couldn't imagine a paddle boat on this river, but the old timers did amazing things. I never saw it again. I slowed through the river reaches where it was but gave up and kept going. Soon we encountered an osprey. It flew ahead of us, and we waited for it to land in a tree, but it kept going for a couple turns before it lifted over the trees and disappeared. We frequently encounter ospreys. Two live a turn downriver from the cabin.

I pulled into the mouth of a creek flowing in from the south. White spruce were on both banks, but fifty yards upstream the banks became tall brown reed grass. We'd been here before but were always stopped by logs in the river. The creek ran clear so we putted up the winding waterway, three corners, five corners, fifteen corners until it narrowed to near the width of the boat. I climbed on a bank for a look. The grassland ranged hundreds of acres on both sides of the creek with periodic breaks of willow and birch thickets. I'd been in the grasslands before, too, and knew I couldn't walk across them. The tall toasted grass hid green reeds and linking waterways of ponds and streams. Moose might be in those thickets, though. Using a push pole, I turned the boat around and putted downstream, stopping here and there to cast for grayling.

Back in the main river, I turned again toward the mountains.

"Doylanne, let's plug in the satellite phone while we're running."

About half of the population has never known a world without satellite communications. They've always had the ability to instantly contact anyone. Obviously, the other half have experienced living without it. For those of us in our mid-sixties and beyond, we've lived without computers, cell phones, GPS, the internet, email, texting, Facebook—the list is a book. Telephones in the 1990s were connected by landlines, and those telephones were the pinnacle of personal communications for decades. Before today's instant communication, we went to work in the morning and never thought to call home during the day. Kids who went off to college had telephone budgets. A long-distance telephone call was an expensive activity. People wrote letters to loved ones.

When we first went to the homestead in the late 1980s, there was no expectation of contact. "Talk with you in six weeks," was the message to family and friends. We'd call and we mailed letters before we left Wasilla and when we returned. No one expected more. Our earliest option for communications, one I never used, was a VHF radio with a channel to a jetliner in case of emergency. The idea was to broadcast my call for help and an airliner would pick it up and pass the message along. Might not have worked, but it was hope. For the first half dozen years, we didn't know there was a radio station broadcasting to the area of our cabin. KIAM, a Christian station, reached our area, but we didn't know it. Even one-way communication would have been beneficial, at least a weather forecast. Early on our CB radio enabled communication among ourselves. If I ventured back in the woods or off on a river trip, I could contact Doylanne at the cabin. My first analog cell phone worked for the first fifty miles of the trip.

In 2010 we took a satellite phone on a winter trip, and having the phone likely saved my life. The snowmachine trip wore me out. On the first night at the cabin, I sat upright in bed and called out to the boys. They sprung up, starting the lantern. I squirmed on the bed, suffering a heart attack. Jack called 911 on the satellite phone. He reached the Alaska State Troopers who connected him with the Alaska Air National Guard. We were too remote for a trooper rescue. The Alaska Air National Guard rapidly dispatched an HH-60 Pave Hawk helicopter and HC-130 Hercules aircraft from Anchorage. Facing high winds and a blizzard, the helicopter turned back before reaching the Alaska Range, but the plane kept coming. I heard the aircraft blaze over the cabin about three hours after the initial call. Jack and Jed drove the snowmachines to a clearing about a half mile behind the cabin and shined their lights into the opening. Two pararescue men from the 212th Rescue Squadron jumped into the dark. About 8:00 a.m. an UH-60 helicopter with two pilots, a crew chief, and medic from Fairbank's Fort Wainwright 16th Combat Aviation Brigade hovered over the river. The crew and the boys carried me to the helicopter. I survived because of a phone, intelligent, fast acting sons, amazing medics, skilled and daring pilots, and expert medical care.

Our next technological advance was a handheld device facilitating text messages, GPS, compass navigation, and tracking. By 2018 we had the ability to communicate globally from the river and the cabin.

Now when we go to the woods, a way to communicate

with civilization is considered a necessity. Just a couple decades ago it wasn't. In the past, people lived close to home if they wanted close contact with home. They didn't venture away if they couldn't deal with the separation. This reality has greatly impacted our trips to the wilderness. Decades ago, we took our family with us. Home was where the family was, and the cabin was home. No one followed our trip with satellite driven technology as can be done today. Now Doylanne and I want to be in touch with town, and we are. From the river bank, Doylanne will call a son and messages will be shared among the family with texts and emails. Sometimes the call will be to England to talk with a granddaughter. Communications technology has become essential to our wilderness trips.

Doylanne and I ran on toward the mountains. The river now flowed like a high mountain stream, pebbles visible on the river bottom, the surface mostly ripples and sparkles. There was only one narrow passage suitable for the boat, and my job was to hit it to avoid rocks. The prop sliced rocks. I tilted and trimmed the outboard as high as I could and still allow the water pump to suck water and stay on step. I stopped at another stream.

This golden waterway flowed from the west. Beneath us was a hole where grayling schooled in September. Doylanne and I and all of our sons had fished this spot before and knew what was there. I opened a beer and watched them dimple the surface. Big grayling swam below us. Arctic grayling can live for more than thirty years, and the largest caught have been over five pounds and two feet in length. Below us were fish at least eighteen inches long, not records but big. Doylanne didn't want to fish, but she handled the camera as I caught and released a half dozen.

We left the fishing hole and skimmed upriver through the ripples, the prop kicking up pebbles until I had to stop. The water was gone. I steered over near the bank and putted around another corner. I couldn't go any farther.

"Ready to go back?" I asked.

"Let's get rocks."

I pushed us against a beach. Doylanne picked rocks, looking for the prettiest among the pretty. She had a lot of them to choose from. She made selections based on color, shape, size, and texture. Neither of us knew what kind of rocks were beneath our feet, but we had run the boat into a rock garden. A geologist would know all of these, of course, and might say, "Oh, that's limestone; that's gneiss." In *The Geology of Denali National Park and Preserve*, Michael Collier names rocks found in our river: "Phyllite. Metarhyolite, actinolutic schist, radiolarian, chert, graywacke, Micaceous sandstone, green tuff, serpentinite, gabbro, argillite, granodiorite." Certainly, not an exhaustive list, but some of the many different kinds of rocks found in the rivers flowing on the north side of the Alaska Range. The multicolored stones finished a beautiful waterscape matching the floral landscape of yellow, orange, and red.

"No big rocks here," Doylanne said. The largest we had found in this area were six inches in length, flat and thin. "If we could go farther, we'd probably find big ones." She was right. The big ones haven't tumbled as far and for as long. They were still in the mountains. Downriver, a few miles, even little rocks were hard to find. They had ground to cinnamon-colored sand. This sand would become rock again as it responded to heat and pressure in the next million years or so.

We could see the mountain range from the beach. I wanted to keep going.

"Didn't we go farther last year?" I asked.

"Only a corner."

"Want me to try again?"

"This is far enough."

I walked up the beach, imagining paddling a canoe upstream from this spot. I wasn't sure I could make any progress against the current.

"Guess I need a jet boat," I said.

"Here's a bear track."

A bear had walked to the edge of the stream and turned back. I followed the tracks to the brush.

"A grizzly." I studied the tracks for a few minutes and snapped a couple photos. For years I couldn't tell the difference between a black and a grizzly track. Now I can. A black bear's claws are close to the rounded pad. The square pad on a grizzly track is obviously back away from the claws. "It looks like a fresh track to me."

"I'm done here," Doylanne said. We loaded quickly and I pushed off with the pole, turned the boat around to face downstream, and drifted for thirty minutes to get into deeper water. We cruised toward the cabin. Doylanne put away the satellite phone, now fully charged, and watched for animals.

All journeys are different going back. Like on a curvy country road, every river turn is a mystery. Animals add to the unknown. They make every moment special whether they show themselves or not. Running upstream, animals step back behind foliage when they hear us approach. After we pass, they sometimes come back to the edge. When we run back, they stay in view to see what they missed. Hunters use this as a strategy. One boat runs the river, and thirty minutes later, another boat follows. Sometimes it's the second boat bagging the animal.

We cruised home leaning into the corners. Back at the cabin, Doylanne sorted through a pan of multicolored rocks.

28

Bear on the Trail

"ERIC, HAVE YOU SEEN THE golden ash shovel we brought from England."

"I'll look in the stuff. I'm going to pull out the sawmill."

I faced the mound in the small log cabin we called our shed. I didn't immediately see a golden shovel, but I could see the tip of my sawmill and chainsaw bar poking out from the pile. More than thirty years lay before me: a casing for a lower unit, worn props, tin cans and glass jars of prop washers, nuts and cotter pins, tent spikes, tubes of grease and quarts of oil, spark plugs, water filters, siphoning hose, spool of wire, five- and fifteen-gallon gasoline drums, a rescue floating ring, life vests, two double-edged axes, sledge hammer, screw driver, folded blue poly tarp, mosquito netting, three garden hoses, five-gallon bucket filled with rusty traps, pipe wrench, four-foot length of one-and-a-half-inch well pipe, a tent, straps, a come-a-long, and six hydraulic jacks. Those are the things I could see. My sawmill was beneath most of it. I emptied the cabin, forming another mound on the ground outside.

"Here's the ash shovel."

The chainsaw was still attached to the mill from when I used it in May. I used the deck as a workbench and went through all the bolts on the mill. I also checked the chains. I found a couple sharp ones with ripping teeth. A ripping chain is created by filing the cutting edge of the chain tooth to ten degrees resulting in a blunter edge. This results in a better board than one created with a conventional saw chain. I sharpen my own but don't know if I'm much good at it. I use a power tool made for it, but it took me some time to figure it out. Working on these logs in the woods with bark and dirt, I can get up to a dozen ten-foot cuts with a chain before it must be sharpened.

I ran downstream to the tree I'd fallen before. I used a peavey to roll a section onto a couple short lengths of beaver-killed birch. I cleaned the log with a wire brush and swept it with a broom and placed a nine-foot aluminum guide rail on the top of the log and secured it with dogs (nails attached to the railing are called dogs). I leveled the guide rail. Imagine a log with a runway on its top. The chainsaw and mill, already attached, were placed on the rail, the saw bar lying horizontal. I got in a balanced position, one knee on the ground, fired up the chainsaw, and began the cut. The ripping chain tore into the wood and pulled the saw along. I did my best to keep the railing intact, connected solidly to the log, and mostly level. I stopped midway and placed a wedge behind me to lift the top wood and reduce friction. The cut went well and I was left with a log with a level flat surface. I rotated the log so the flat surface was vertical and installed the railing again. I ended with a two-sided log. I removed the railing and used one of the flat sides for the sawmill. I adjusted the mill to two inches and cut slices.

It takes lots of boards, so I moved on to the next log. I cut boards, dropped more trees, and cut more boards for two weeks, until I had enough. Doylanne helped me haul them to the boat and up the bank to the lumber yard at the cabin.

With Doylanne's help, we used a table saw to make dimensional lumber that turned out close enough.

"Done," I said.

"Enough?"

"Maybe."

"What should we do now?"

"Build a shed."

I'll refrain from a step by step shed-building tutorial. They're everywhere. It took me a week to use up the boards, but a proper shed fully enclosed with a door and a latch stood before us. The construction was pretty standard with floor joists, studs, rafters, and green metal roofing brought in through the years, but there were no holes dug through the active layer.

"The shed's nice, Eric," Doylanne said.

I put stuff in its place. It's remarkable how much fun it all is when the work is done. A woodpecker started up behind the shed. I stepped in the trees and saw it. Good-sized bird with a white streak backward from its eyes and a red patch on its head called to me. It was time to hike back in the woods again.

"Let's try to get a moose. I'll go to King Beaver tonight and watch. Want to come along? I can get a moose out of there."

"I'll stay here. Take a walkie-talkie."

I went to King Beaver Pond and crept to the edge of the ridge overlooking the water. I sat against a white spruce and glassed and imagined a moose appearing at any moment. After all the years, I'd never shot a moose at King Beaver, but I had a plan. I settled back against the tree and closed my eyes and rested, glassed, rested, and dreamed. A breeze from the south stirred the pond water and a beaver emerged, heading toward his home with a birch branch in its mouth.

Perhaps billionaires are like beavers. They live in beautiful lodges with spectacular waterfront views but are never done. They've never accomplished enough, built enough, gathered enough. To a beaver, trees are for the taking, so they take them, whether they need them or not. It's a disorder. The beaver dove to the right of the massive beaver lodge standing ten feet or so above the water line with a circumference of more than twenty feet. I saw a limousine parked in front and two doormen standing near a glass entry. A woman holding a long slender glass stood on a third-story balcony. The beaver resurfaced near the doormen. I opened my eyes.

An hour later, at the edge of darkness, my walkie-talkie belched. The radio, tucked in a front pocket of my coat, sounded again before I could get to it, so I grabbed my gear and headed quickly away from the ridge. I didn't want the sound to scare away a moose. Out of view of the pond, I knelt in a patch of cranberries and pulled out the radio and called Doylanne. She responded in a burst, but the only words I recognized were bear on trail. My trail? I put away the radio and checked my rifle. One round in the chamber, two in the magazine. I headed up the trail toward the cabin. I was walking in the dark again. My face had mostly healed. I heard a snap ahead of me. I crouched. A trail here is not a pathway; it's an animal trail. Leaves rustled. Something moved out there in the black, something creepy like there always was when walking home in the dark as a kid along an unlit street, or years later, when a school principal, inching through a pitch-black forty-thousand-square-foot school, feeling my way through the hallways. I was catching nyctophobia, if catching it is how you get it.

I took a deep breath, wiped my forehead, and stared into darkness. Bears see well in the dark. I couldn't see anything beyond the short beam of my headlamp. I wanted out of there. I took off on the trail, branches from birch and willow reaching for me. A large fallen spruce lay across the trail. Go over or under? I crawled over and stopped. I heard steps, had to be steps, behind me.

"Eric," Doylanne yelled. I reached the edge of the clearing and saw the lunar module and Doylanne's silhouette holding a lantern. I scanned the yard and waited for black stumps to move.

Temperatures dropped below freezing most nights in late September, and we were headed where it was time for the going if we hoped to get out in a boat. I sat exhausted near the stove with a beer and book.

"It's time to go home, Doylanne. I dodged a bear, and the river will soon begin freezing."

29

Steinbeck

I THOUGHT OF THE YEAR BEFORE, late September, when Doylanne and I hauled ourselves into the cabin near dark. We'd been out all day looking for a moose. We hiked where we shouldn't have, climbed slippery river banks, and trudged over muskeg. Icy rain stung our faces during the boat ride back to the cabin. I'd hit the wall. Exhausted, hungry, and getting old, I sunk into my chair at the dining table, and the heat from the woodstove poured over me. Doylanne draped clothing near the stove. I read from John Steinbeck's *The Red Pony*: "When the peaks were pink in the morning, they invited him among them: and when the sun had gone over the edge in the evening and the mountains were a purple-like despair, then Jody was afraid of them; then they were so impersonal and aloof that their very imperturbability was a threat."

On dreary evenings, when I'm tired and sore, I look to a beloved story or favorite author. For me, when I know I've had to fight a bit during the day, it's often Steinbeck. I don't know much about him, but I've read his books during murky, burdensome times after I've had to toughen-up to get through the day. I keep Steinbeck at the cabin. There is honor, I think, in facing the hardest days with defiance, a message I get from Steinbeck. At times I think I could wedge my way into *East of Eden, Cannery Row, Tortilla Flat, Grapes of Wrath, The Wayward Bus, The Red Pony*, and *Of Mice and Men* and know I'm right at home. Over the years I have met others who could have filled a role in a Steinbeck story. Perhaps that was Steinbeck's genius. Most of us have been there. Embattled days lead us to where we seek comfort. On those besieged days, scattered and always unwelcomed, relief is found on a simple paper birch split-log bookshelf in a small log cabin under the canopy of saturated and dripping white spruce.

I read *The Red Pony* again.

"I'll hunt a few more days before we go," I said.

I sat on meadows, leaned against trees, climbed tree stands, drifted the river. I hunted until dark, starting in the frosty mornings. I heard moose but none showed. On the twenty-third day of the trip, the last day of the hunting season, we left for town.

Going Home

30

Hourglass

The boat sat several inches higher in the river with our light load. Camping gear, sixty gallons of gasoline, and a few white spruce boards for a bookshelf project in town comprised the load. I placed the rifle in the bow. There might be a moose yet. Craig Childs in *The Animal Dialogues* describes encounters with animals like this: "You will see things, even if you are not looking. You come out and the animals will find you, even if you never knew they were there." Animals found us, not the other way around. Bears came to our cabin, squirrels, woodpeckers, and owls announced their locations. It was time for a moose to come to us. They often did. I motored a short ways upstream, above the cabin so we could be there a bit longer. I anticipated two days on the river, maybe a moose.

We headed home. On a river turn where the sun shot through a break in the clouds blinding me, I turned onto a sand bar the boat slid abruptly to a stop.

You run enough rivers you know when you're stuck. We were stuck. The earth had us like a fly catcher. Doylanne handed me chest waders and I grumbled. I stepped off into the water and the boat rose a little. I knew immediately we were okay but work lay ahead before we floated again. Doylanne would have to get out too. We called this a Code 4. We had codes for degrees of the earth's stickiness. Glide to a half but working a push pole could move the boat was a Code 1. Grind to a stop but I could push the boat if I got out, Code 2. If it took both of us out and pushing to move the boat, Code 3. We both got out and with the aid of equipment could move the boat, Code 4. We were a Code 4. Both of us pushing could not move the boat, so I used a farm jack to lift one side of the boat a few inches, allowing water to flow beneath, and we pushed. We'd go a few inches or a foot. We'd make it. When we were close to a stronger current and likely drop-off, Doylanne tried to climb into the boat but couldn't wrestle herself over the gunwale. I hustled around the aft to her side as the boat began to move on its own. I lifted and she pulled herself in.

Seconds later sand disappeared beneath my feet. I pulled myself high enough to keep the water from filling my chest waders. Doylanne pulled on me but I wasn't moving. I hung from the side of the boat.

"Start the boat and pull away from the sweepers." She shook her head. "Do it. Go slow." She started the motor but the lower unit was out of the water. I'd raised it while we were stuck. She knew the sound of the propeller twirling in the air so lowered the prop. The boat surged forward, and she steered toward the middle. She turned off the engine and came back to me. I lifted my right foot to the gunwale and Doylanne pulled on my foot. We moved again in inches. My knee passed the edge, and she hauled me into the boat.

We putted in the current, replaying those seconds. I did it again, pushed it too far, too long. We ran silent into the afternoon, pulling to a beach near dark to camp. I watched for a moose but didn't walk back to the meadow a few hundred feet through the willows.

We lay in the moonlight in our bags. "Eric, we were coming up with ways to keep making this trip possible," Doylanne said. She turned off the lantern. "If you drown or get lost in the woods, it doesn't work."

A strip of moonlight crossed Doylanne, and I followed it two hundred and thirty-nine thousand miles. If I watched long enough, the light would transform the night and alter my feelings. Doylanne's breathing changed to sleeping. I closed my eyes and built a list of the topics we talked about during the month: supplies and equipment, decision-making abilities, senses in a wilderness landscape, failing physical capabilities, declining spatial awareness, purpose and motivation, physical health, and communication technology. I ran through the list again and again and fell asleep with an arm over Doylanne.

I'd recovered by morning. We left the beach after heating coffee water with the biomass stove and the fog broke enough to see. Minutes later I ran aground.

"Eric?"

I pushed us off the edge and into the current with the pole—only a Code 1. We cruised on, the sky improving.

I stopped for a break on the corner where I'd found the grave marker years before. A single mosquito flew around my head and landed on my right cheek below my eye. I waited for it to puncture me, but I didn't feel anything. Doylanne brushed it away. I hadn't seen one of those in several hours, and I soon wouldn't see another for several months. The cross lay on the ground face-down among rose hips, so I propped it against a spruce. Maybe this will be me one day. I imagined leaves swirling at the end of autumn and hunters walking the property, examining the cabin and the outbuildings. They would find my grave, read the inscription on the copper plate, and spend a few moments lost in the dark autumn forest with its reaching arms and peering eyes while a river ran away with time.

"Doylanne, look for an hourglass in town. I want one of those at the cabin."

Twice we've been present when a river changed course—changed direction completely. The first time was in the early 1990s during Doylanne's first trip to the cabin. The other time occurred on this trip back to town.

On the lower end of the river, cruising about twenty-five miles an hour, I veered hard right with the current into the woods with broken trees lining the edges. More accurately, the river pulled us into the channel. There seemed little choice. We both sat erect. Doylanne gripped the dash. The boat careened into a narrow opening of rushing water. Spears broke the water surface and debris disappeared in maelstroms. I slowed but had to maintain good speed to keep control of the boat. We swerved through logs and lances in the bottleneck for several hundred yards until we reconnected with the other side, the main river course.

The river changed its mind and didn't warn us. We circled when we emerged from the trees and studied the new channel, what would become our new way.

"Doylanne, when do you think you've been the happiest?" She searched in the cooler for crackers.

"Random question."

"What do you think?"

"I don't know. I'm probably most content now. Life has slowed some."

We turned onto another river, an upstream run of more than eighty miles, little wind, the water smooth. The fog dissolved, revealing a brilliant sky. Frost covered six white spruce boards stacked in the bow. On a long stretch of river with banks of drab spruce, Doylanne pointed to a rainbow. "There's some more color," she said.

"What do you see?"

"Red, green, orange, and blue."

"Yeah, red, green. I see yellow, lots of yellow."

"I don't see the yellow."

"No two people see the same rainbow. I've been thinking about your dream at the train station."

"Train station? Didn't we talk about the train station dream months ago."

"I remember King's Cross. From the moment we began our journey, there was no stopping. We were pulled along, with little control, like what happened just now in the river. The sand can't stop itself in an hourglass, and neither can we refrain from following moose too far near dark or end our dreams of cabins and sheds. We just get pulled along like the old man in the sea."

"Maybe we are too old, Eric."

We shared crackers and cookies and took our morning medication.

"No, not yet, but I do need to act my age."

"We can hope. I love the shed, Eric."

Eric Wade is a writer, teacher, musician, naturalist, and outdoorsman. He earned a bachelors in English Education at Southern Oregon University and a masters in Journalism from the University of Oregon. He served as a public-school teacher, principal, and director of nonprofit corporations for more than forty years. He often journeys into the Alaska interior wilderness where he roams the woods looking for wildlife—flora and fauna—as it's always been. He is the author of *Cabin: An Alaska Wilderness Dream*, 2019.

Doylanne Wade can dash for a camera with lightning speed, a skill she honed chasing four sons. When wild animals appear or sunsets morph to mesmerizing beauty, there's often little time to respond, an aspect of photography she loves. For more than thirty years, she has captured stories in the Alaska wilderness. She uses a DSLR camera with 150-600mm and 18-270 lenses.

Lightning Source UK Ltd.
Milton Keynes UK
UKHW022313040222
398230UK00008B/359